How to Manage

PEARSON

At Pearson, we believe in learning – all kinds of learning for all kinds of people. Whether it's at home, in the classroom or in the workplace, learning is the key to improving our life chances.

That's why we're working with leading authors to bring you the latest thinking and best practices, so you can get better at the things that are important to you. You can learn on the page or on the move, and with content that's always crafted to help you understand quickly and apply what you've learned.

If you want to upgrade your personal skills or accelerate your career, become a more effective leader or more powerful communicator, discover new opportunities or simply find more inspiration, we can help you make progress in your work and life.

Pearson is the world's leading learning company. Our portfolio includes the Financial Times and our education business, Pearson International.

Every day our work helps learning flourish, and wherever learning flourishes, so do people.

To learn more, please visit us at **www.pearson.com/uk**

How to Manage

The definitive guide to effective management

4th edition

Jo Owen

PEARSON

Harlow, England • London • New York • Boston • San Francisco • Toronto • Sydney
Auckland • Singapore • Hong Kong • Tokyo • Seoul • Taipei • New Delhi
Cape Town • São Paulo • Mexico City • Madrid • Amsterdam • Munich • Paris • Milan

PEARSON EDUCATION LIMITED
Edinburgh Gate
Harlow CM20 2JE
United Kingdom
Tel: +44 (0)1279 623623
Web: www.pearson.com/uk

First published in Great Britain in 2006 (print and electronic)
Second edition published 2009 (print and electronic)
Third edition published 2012 (print and electronic)
Fourth edition published 2015 (print and electronic)

Pearson Education is not responsible for the content of third-party internet sites.

ISBN: 978-1-292-08366-7 (print)
        978-1-292-08368-1 (PDF)
        978-1-292-08367-4 (eText)
        978-1-292-08369-8 (ePub)

British Library Cataloguing-in-Publication Data
A catalogue record for the print edition is available from the British Library

Library of Congress Cataloging-in-Publication Data
A catalog record for the print edition is available from the Library of Congress

10 9 8 7 6 5 4 3 2 1
19 18 17 16 15

Cover design by Nick Redeyoff

Print edition typeset in 10/14 Plantin by 76
Print edition printed by Ashford Colour Press Ltd, Gosport

NOTE THAT ANY PAGE CROSS REFERENCES REFER TO THE PRINT EDITION

Contents

About the author

Jo Owen practices what he preaches as a leader. He has worked with over 100 of the best (and one or two of the worst) organisations on the planet. He was a partner at Accenture and started a bank.

He is a founder of eight charities with a combined turnover of over £100 million annually, including Teach First which is the largest graduate recruiter in the UK. Jo is a top corporate coach and speaker on leadership, and is the bestselling author of *How to Lead, How to Sell, How to Influence* and *The Mobile MBA*. He can be reached at jo@ilead.guru.

About the fourth edition

How to Manage remains the classic text on building the rational, political and emotional skills you need to succeed.

Books, like managers, must keep learning, growing and moving ahead if they are to stay relevant. Since *How to Manage* was first published, I have received many helpful suggestions on topics readers would like to see included; I have also received many stories and ideas. My only regret is that I cannot include all the material and ideas submitted. But there are some important areas that are covered with wholly original material in this edition, including:

● managing your career
● managing yourself: finding your peak performance zone and staying there
● becoming the leader your team wants to follow
● becoming influential across your organisation
● managing difficult people, including your boss.

In addition, recent research has shown that the best managers act differently because they think differently. This mindset is predictable, consistent and anyone can learn it. A new section summarises the results of my original research in this area.

I have also responded to reader requests to summarise key points in simple checklists, which you can copy, take away or hand out to colleagues. You will find 30 of these checklists split between this edition of *How to Manage* and its sister book *How to Lead* (fourth edition).

These cover all the topics that managers have to master, including driving performance, managing time, setting and controlling budgets, dealing with crises and delegating.

In addition to these changes, I have reviewed the whole book and updated stories and cases, and included new ones where appropriate. Recognising that your time is at a premium, I have also condensed as many chapters as possible, which creates space for some of the new material.

Taken in isolation, each one of these changes is incremental. The fundamental message and framework of *How to Manage* has not changed: the best managers have the right combination of intelligence quotient (IQ), emotional quotient (EQ) and political quotient (PQ). But, taken together, these changes mark a significant step forwards, which I hope you will enjoy and find useful.

How to Manage is not a theory of management. It is successful management, as anyone can practise it.

Chapter 1

Introduction and summary:
real managers for the real world

Management used to be much simpler: bosses bossed and workers worked. Managers used their heads and workers used their hands. Thinking and doing were separate activities. Those were good times for managers, but bad times for workers.

Somewhere, it all started to go horribly wrong for managers. Workers slowly acquired more rights while managers lost their perks; workers got shorter working hours, managers had to work even longer hours. And while workers got the benefits of the 24/7 economy, managers got the stress of being constantly shackled to the electronic fetters of email, texts and phone.

Management has become harder. It has also become more ambiguous. Think for a moment about the rules of success and survival in your organisation. You can look in vain at the formal evaluation criteria to find the real rules of survival and success:

- How much risk should I take if I want to survive, and how much should I take if I want to succeed?
- What are the right projects and people to work with?
- When do I stand up and fight and when do I concede gracefully?
- How do things actually get done in this place?
- What are the bear traps to avoid?
- How do I manage my boss?

There is no policy manual to tell you this, no training programme to help you. Bosses do not come with a user guide or guarantee. You are on your own when it comes to the important rules. Policies deal only with the minor rules.

In practice, we discover the rules of survival and success by comparing people who succeed and survive to those who struggle. And then we work out why they succeed, survive or struggle. Take a look and see who succeeds where you work. Hopefully, people who have a track record of success are among the winners. But in flat organisations, knowing who was really responsible for what can be a challenge.

Most evaluation systems look for two sorts of characteristics, which are called many different things.

Traditionally, managers (who had the brains) were meant to be smarter than the workers (who had the hands). A good IQ, or intelligence quotient, helped. Many assessment systems still assess IQ. Entry into many business schools is still based on IQ, in the form of the GMAT (a common test). In companies, IQ often is presented as having problem-solving skills, analytical capability, business judgement and insight.

> Being a brain on a stick is not enough; managing is about making things happen through other people.

Being a brain on a stick is not enough; managing is about making things happen through other people. Many smart people with a high IQ are too clever to make anything happen. Most companies also look for good interpersonal skills, or good EQ (emotional quotient). This will be dressed up as teamwork, adaptability, interpersonal effectiveness, charisma, ability to motivate and similar code words for EQ.

Now use the criteria of IQ and EQ to see who succeeds and fails. Look around your workplace. You should find quite a few managers with good IQ and EQ: smart (IQ) and nice (EQ) managers exist, despite the media stereotypes. But you will also find plenty of smart and nice people who lead lives of quiet under-achievement in the backwaters of the organisation: liked by all and going nowhere fast. Meanwhile, there are plenty of successful managers who are not so smart and not so nice who rise to the top, using the smart and nice managers as doormats on their way to the top.

Something is missing. It helps to have good IQ and EQ, but it is not enough. Another hurdle has come into place for managers to jump. As ever, things are getting tougher, not easier, for managers.

The new hurdle is about political savvy or PQ – political quotient. PQ is partly about knowing how to acquire power. Even more, it involves knowing how to use power to make things happen. This places it at the heart of management, which is about making things happen through other people.

Of course, all managers have always needed some degree of PQ. But in the command and control hierarchies of the past, it did not require much PQ to make things happen: an order was normally enough. In today's world of flat and matrix organisations, power is more diffused and ambiguous. If management used to be about making things happen through other people, now it is about making things happen through people you may not control and may not even like. If there is a revolution in management, it is not about technology: the technology revolution has been with us for at least two hundred years. The management revolution is about how you have to make things happen in a far more complicated, difficult and ambiguous world than before.

Making things happen means that you have to build alliances, seek help and support and reach out beyond your formal areas of authority. Many of the resources you need may not even exist in your own organisation. Managers need PQ more than ever before to achieve their ends.

Successful managers are three dimensional: they have IQ, EQ and PQ. Each of these capabilities is a series of skills which can be learned. You do not have to be academically smart to be a good manager: many academic institutions are full of smart people and bad management. *How to Manage* shows how you can be managerially smart without having to be academically smart. Similarly, EQ and PQ represent skills that all managers can learn.

How to Manage lays out the managerial skills behind IQ, EQ and PQ. It shows how you can build your capabilities to survive and succeed in the management revolution. It cuts through the noise of the daily management struggle and the babble of management theory to focus on the critical skills and interventions managers need. It shows what you have to do and how you have to do it in a world that is tougher and more complex than ever.

As a first step in understanding the revolution, we will look at how the revolution came about and where it is taking us.

1.1 Rational management

As long as there has been civilisation, there has been management – even if no one realised it at the time. Management started to evolve as a discipline in its own right with the Industrial Revolution: large-scale operations required large-scale organisation. Early management organisation and strategy was based on military strategy and organisation: classic command and control.

Slowly, industrial management evolved away from military management. Just as Newton discovered the laws of physics, so managers went in search of the elusive formula for business and management success. It is a formula that academics still search for, although successful entrepreneurs do not need a theory to succeed. Scientific Management was an early attempt to bottle success.

The high priest of Scientific Management was Frederick Taylor, who wrote *The Principles of Scientific Management* in 1911. Below is a flavour of his approach:

> *One of the very first requirements for a man who is fit to handle pig iron as a regular occupation is that he shall be so stupid and so phlegmatic that he more nearly resembles in his mental make-up the ox than any other type. The man who is mentally alert and intelligent is for this very reason entirely unsuited to what would, for him, be the grinding monotony of work of this character.*

Taylor took a dim view of workers as a whole, believing that they would work as little as they could without getting punished. But his work was not based on pure opinion: it was also supported by close observation. This led to some ideas that were revolutionary at the time:

- Workers were allowed to rest because it made them more productive.
- Different types of people should be given different types of job because they would be more productive in the right jobs.
- Production lines, which break up complicated jobs such as assembling cars or fast food, maximise productivity and minimise the skills and costs of the employees required.

These lessons are applied still today.

The world of scientific, or rational, management was brought to life by Henry Ford's introduction of the moving production line for making cars. Between 1908 and 1913 he perfected the concept and started to produce the Model T, which he called with great marketing aplomb 'a motor car for the great multitude'. Some 15 million Model Ts had rolled off his assembly lines by 1927, bringing cars to the masses and sweeping away the cottage industry of craftsmen custom building cars at great expense.

Rational management is alive and kicking, even in the twenty-first century: it still exists on car assembly lines, in fast-food restaurants and in call centres where hapless operatives work to scripts that make them little more than machines. Many companies have taken the next logical step and removed the humans completely so that customers are left talking to computers.

1.2 Emotional management

The world of rational, scientific management was relatively simple: it was based on observation and cold calculation.

Then it all started becoming complicated for managers.

Somewhere along the line, someone discovered that workers were not mere units of production, and possibly even of consumption. They had hopes, fears, feelings and even the occasional thought. They were, in fact, human beings. This really confused matters for managers. They not only had to handle problems, they also had to handle people.

Over time, people became harder to handle. Workers became better educated and better skilled: they could now contribute more, but they also expected more. They became wealthier and more independent. The days of the one-factory town were numbered: there were alternative forms of employment. The Welfare State emerged for those who could not or would not find employment. Employers lost their coercive power. They could no longer demand loyalty; they had to earn it. Slowly, the workplace was moving from a culture of compliance to a culture of commitment.

The challenge for management was to produce the high-commitment workplace, engaging people's hopes instead of simply playing on their fears. Eighty-four years after Frederick Taylor published his book, Daniel Goleman appeared as the high priest of the new world of emotional management with *Emotional Intelligence: Why it can matter more than IQ* (1995). He was, in effect, popularising thinking, which had been emerging for decades. As early as 1920, E.L. Thorndike of Columbia University had been writing about 'social intelligence'. For a long time, thinkers had realised that smart thinking (high IQ) was not correlated directly with life success: other things seem to be important.

In the workplace, experiments with emotional intelligence (EQ, not IQ) had long been taking place. The Japanese, in particular, made great strides in involving workers properly, even on car production lines, through new movements such as *kaizen* (continuous improvement). Perhaps, ironically, they took much of their inspiration from an American, W. Edwards Deming. Deming's ideas gained acceptance in America only when the Japanese started to decimate the American auto industry with the help of his ideas.

By the end of the twentieth century, the manager's job had become far more complicated than it had been at the end of the nineteenth century. Twentieth-century managers needed to be just as smart as their predecessors of a hundred years before. They needed EQ (emotional quotient) to deal with people as much as they needed IQ to deal with problems. Most managers found that they could be good at one or the other: few managers have genuinely good IQ *and* EQ. The performance bar for effective management had been raised dramatically.

1.3 Political management

Two-dimensional managers cannot exist, except as cartoon characters. Real people and real managers exist in three dimensions. The concepts of high IQ and EQ are good, but they are not sufficient to explain the success or otherwise of different sorts of managers. Something is missing.

The first clue to finding the missing piece of the puzzle is to recognise that organisations are set up for conflict. This is a surprise to many academics who think that organisations are set up for collaboration. In reality, managers have to fight for a limited pot of their organisation's time, money and budget. There are always more needs than there are resources. Internal conflict is the way that these priorities are decided. Marketing, operations, service, HR and the different products and regions all slug it out to get their fair share of the cake.

> For many managers, the real competition is not in the marketplace but sitting at a hot desk nearby, fighting for the same promotion and the same bonus pool.

For many managers, the real competition is not in the marketplace but sitting at a hot desk nearby, fighting for the same promotion and the same bonus pool.

The second clue to the missing piece of the puzzle is to look at who wins and loses in these corporate contests for budget, time, pay and promotion. If we are to believe the high IQ and EQ theory, then all the smart and nice people should get to the top. Casual observation of most organisations shows that this is not true. Smart and nice people do not always win: many disappear off the corporate radar screen entirely or live as quiet under-achievers. On the other side of the coin, most of us have experienced senior managers who are neither bright nor pleasant, and yet they rise mysteriously into positions of power and prominence.

Clearly, there is something more than IQ and EQ.

A short chat around the water cooler often is enough to discover what is missing. Around the water cooler, conversation often turns to who is going up or down the corporate escalator, who is in and out, who is doing what to whom, what the big emerging opportunities are, and what the emerging Death Star projects are and how to avoid them. Such conversations show that humans are not only social animals: we are also political animals.

Politics is unavoidable in any organisation. Nor is politics new. Shakespeare's *Julius Caesar* is politics dramatised. Machiavelli's

The Prince is the Renaissance guide to successful political management. Politics has always been there, but it has been seen as a slightly dirty topic, not fit for academic analysis or for corporate training programmes. Caesar's murder shows what happens when you do not read the politics well. When anyone says, as Brutus said to Caesar, 'I'm right behind you', alert managers realise that this means they are about to be stabbed in the back.

For some, politics is a malign force and it is about back stabbing. For more effective managers, it is a benign force. PQ is the art of making the organisation work with you and for you. It is how you make things happen through parts of the organisation you do not control. That puts it at the heart of modern management, where managers find that they do not control all the resources they need for success.

IQ and EQ are not sufficient to deal with such politics. There is a constant contest for control and for power. The endless need for change is not just about changing individuals: it is about changing the power balance in the organisation. These are deeply political acts for which the successful manager needs deep political and organisational skills.

The importance of politics is growing and will keep on growing, because the nature of management itself is changing. Over the last 20 years there has been a slow-motion revolution in management. From day to day you cannot see the revolution, unless it sweeps you away in a blitz of outsourcing, offshoring and re-engineering. But over 20 years, it is clear that the old order is vanishing and a new order is emerging.

The old order was based on command and control. The job of a manager was to transmit orders down the command chain, and to send messages back up it. Effective managers made things happen through the people they controlled.

Because managers no longer control all the resources they need in order to make things happen, that changes everything. Effective managers have to make things happen through people they do not control, and may not even like. Traditional command and control just does not work in this world: you cannot simply order your peers, colleagues, customers and bosses to do what you say. You have to learn a whole new set of skills around influencing, persuading, building networks of trust, securing resources and teams and making things happen without formal power: that is the real world of PQ.

Clearly, some managers and some organisations are still in the old world of command and control. But the tide is moving against those ways of working, even in the public sector. If you want to thrive, make sure you are on the right side of the revolution. Acquire the PQ skills that will let you flourish in a world that is becoming more complicated, more ambiguous and, yet, has more opportunity than ever.

1.4 Management quotient

Perhaps it is now time to recognise that real managers are three-dimensional. In addition to high IQ and EQ, they need high PQ: political quotient. If there is such a thing as a success formula in management, it might be summarised as:

$$MQ = IQ + EQ + PQ$$

MQ is your management quotient. To increase your MQ, you need to build up IQ, EQ and PQ (see the figure opposite). The success formula is easy to state, hard to achieve.

MQ is about management practice, not management theory. *How to Manage* shows how you can use MQ as a simple framework to:

- assess your own management potential
- assess team members and help them identify how they can improve
- identify and build the core skills you need to succeed
- identify the rules of survival and success in your organisation.

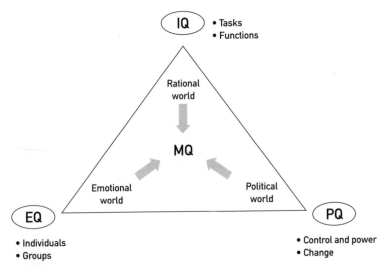

Components of MQ

There are countless ways to apply the MQ formula and to succeed or to fail. Each person develops and applies IQ, EQ and PQ in different ways to suit different situations. Each person's management style is as unique as their DNA. *How to Manage* does not provide a formula for producing managerial clones. You deserve better than that. It provides a set of frameworks and tools to help you understand and deal with typical management challenges.

Some people treat frameworks as prisons: they mindlessly apply the same formula to every situation. Others use frameworks as scaffolding around which they can build their own unique management style. They adapt the tools to their particular circumstances. *How to Manage* helps you adapt the tools and frameworks by showing not just the theory, but also the reality of what works and, more importantly, what does not work. We all learn from experience, both positive and negative. This book crams thousands of years of cumulative experience from practising managers into a few pages. Use *How to Manage* well and you will be able to build your MQ to succeed on your own terms.

Chapter 2

Rational management skills:

dealing with problems, tasks and money

B eing a smart manager is different from being a smart intellectual. Brilliant professors rarely emerge as great managers. Conversely, many of the best entrepreneurs today are college dropouts. Bill Gates, Lawrence Ellison, Li Ka-shing, Mark Zuckerberg and Amancio Ortega have all made billions without the need for a degree. They are all among the top 20 richest people in the world.

Asking great managers what makes them great is an exercise in toadying and ingratiation that yields little more than platitudes and self-congratulation. I have tried it: it is not an exercise worth doing once, let alone repeating. For the most part, they will talk about things like experience and intuition. This is deeply unhelpful. You cannot teach intuition. Experience is a recipe for keeping junior managers junior until they have grown enough grey hairs to become part of the management club. I had to find out another way of discovering how managers thought, short of wiring them up to machines all day. So I did the next best thing: I decided to watch them work. Watching people work invariably is more congenial than actually doing the work.

Each person and each day is unique. Some people prefer face-to-face work rather than dealing through email; some days are totally consumed by a couple of big meetings; some people work longer and a few work less. But once we stripped away all these variances, we found these familiar patterns to a manager's working day:

- high fragmentation of time
- management of multiple and competing agendas
- management of multiple constituencies
- constant flow of new information requiring reaction, change, adjustment
- low amounts of time working alone.

This is a pattern that is familiar to most managers. It has been compared to juggling while trying to run a marathon in a series of 100-metre sprints without dropping any of the balls. It is a world in which it is very easy to be busy but very difficult to make an impact. Activity is not a substitute for achievement. The challenge for managers today is to do less and achieve more.

> Activity is not a substitute for achievement.

At this point, pause to consider what you do not see in the normal management day:

- decision making, using formal tools, such as Bayesian analysis and decision trees
- problem solving, either by sitting alone and thinking deeply or by working in a group with a formal problem-solving technique
- formal strategic analysis of the business.

Many MBA tools are notable by their absence from the daily lives of most managers: organisational and strategic theory go missing; financial and accounting tools remain functionally isolated within finance and accounting; marketing remains a mystery to most people in operations or IT.

The absence of these tools from most managers' days does not make them irrelevant. They may be used sparingly, but at critical moments.

Most organisations would not survive long if all their managers were conducting non-stop strategic reviews of the business. But a good strategic review once in five years by the CEO can transform the business.

By now my search for the art of management was becoming lost in the whirl of activity that is the standard management day. It looked like great managers did not need to be intellectually smart and did not need the standard intellectual and analytical tools that appear in books and courses. But it would be a brave person who accused Bill Gates and Richard Branson of being dumb. All the leaders and managers we interviewed were smart enough to get into positions of power and influence. They were smart, but not in the conventional way of schools. Management intelligence is different from academic intelligence.

We decided to dig deeper, thereby breaking the golden rule 'when in a hole, stop digging'. We hoped we were not digging a hole. We hoped we were digging the foundations of understanding the management mindset. Eventually, we found these foundations – explored in the following sections of this chapter – all of which can be learned and acquired by any manager:

Starting at the end: focus on outcomes

Achieving results: performance and perceptions

Making decisions: acquiring intuition fast

Solving problems: prisons and frameworks – and tools

Strategic thinking: floors, romantics and the classics

Setting budgets: the politics of performance

Managing budgets: the annual dance routine

Managing costs: minimising pain

Surviving spreadsheets: assumptions, not maths

Knowing numbers: playing the numbers game

If we were being intellectually rigorous, not all of these skills might exist in a chapter on management IQ. But there is some method behind the randomness.

Outcome focus and achieving results (Starting at the end and Achieving results) are included in this chapter because they are at the heart of the effective manager's mindset. The way an effective manager thinks is driven by the need to drive results and achieve outcomes. This creates a style of thinking that is highly pragmatic, fast-paced and quite unlike anything you find normally in textbooks and academia. It is about achievement, not activity.

Making decisions, Solving problems and Strategic thinking are classic IQ skills. There is a huge difference between how textbooks say managers should think and how they really think. Textbooks look for the perfect answer. The perfect solution is the enemy of the practical solution. Searching for perfection leads to inaction. Practical solutions lead to what good managers want: action. For many managers, the real problem is not even finding the answer: the real challenge is finding out the question. The really good managers spend more time working out what the question is, before attempting to find the pragmatic answer.

> The perfect solution is the enemy of the practical solution.

Setting budgets, Managing budgets, Managing costs, Surviving spreadsheets and Knowing numbers could be called FQ – financial quotient. We expected to find that finance and accounting is 100 per cent IQ. We were 100 per cent wrong. In theory, financial management is a highly objective and intellectual exercise in which answers are either right or wrong: the numbers do or do not add up. For managers, the intellectual challenge is the minor part of the challenge. The major part of the challenge is not intellectual: it is political. Most financial discussions and negotiations are political discussions about money, power, resources, commitments and expectations. In many ways, financial management could belong better in the PQ (political quotient) chapter. Out of deference to financial theory, it is included in this, the IQ chapter.

In the sections that follow, we will pay our dues to theory. Theory is not useless: good theory creates a framework for structuring and understanding unstructured and complex issues. The main focus, however, is on the method of how managers develop and deploy these IQ skills in practice.

2.1 Starting at the end: focus on outcomes

Managers have long been told 'first things first'. This is tautological nonsense: it depends on what you define as 'first'. In practice, managers do not start at the start. Effective managers start at the end.

For speed readers, let's repeat the message: *effective managers start at the end.*

Working backwards from the desired outcome, rather than shambling forwards from today, is at the heart of how good managers think and work. This outcome focus is essential because it achieves the following:

- creates clarity and focuses on what is important
- pushes people to action, not analysis
- finds positive ways forward, rather than worrying about the past
- simplifies priorities
- helps to identify potential obstacles and avoid them.

Outcome focus is a relatively easy discipline to learn. It requires asking the same four questions time and time again:

1   What outcome do I want to achieve from this situation?
2   What outcome does the other person expect from this situation?
3   What are the minimum number of steps required to get there?
4   What are the consequences of this course of action?

Keep asking these four questions relentlessly and you will find the fog of confusion lifts from most situations, and you can drive a team to action.

1 What outcome do I want to achieve from this situation?

Asking this question drives us into action and gives people a sense of clarity and purpose. It is also a way of taking control of a situation and gaining benefit from it. It is a way of avoiding becoming dependent on other people's agendas, being purely reactive, or of slipping into analysis paralysis. Two examples will make the point:

Example one

A project was going horribly wrong: it threatened to go over time and budget. The team was having an inquest, which rapidly was turning into the normal blame game of 'he said… she said… I said no, she said…' Things were turning nasty. Then the team leader stopped the debate and asked: 'OK, we have two weeks left on the project. The question is this: what can we do in the next two weeks to achieve a satisfactory outcome?' Suddenly, the debate turned from defensive analysis into a positive discussion about what the team could do. The leader had focused the team on outcomes and action, not on problems and analysis.

Example two

The analyst had done a great job. She had compiled a mountain of data. The result was that her draft presentation was indigestible. Every piece of data was so good it was hard to see what to leave out. So her manager asked her to focus on what she wanted to achieve from the presentation. The desired outcome was very simple: agree to a new project. Suddenly, it was easy to focus on a short storyline that could persuade the decision maker about the project. The discussion was no longer 'what shall we leave out of the presentation?' but 'what is the minimum we need to include to make our case?' About 90 per cent of the presentation disappeared into an appendix that was never read. The analyst had learned that presentations and reports are not complete when there is nothing left to say or write: they are complete only when it is impossible to say or write any less. Brevity is much harder than length. Presentations and reports are like diamonds: they benefit greatly from good cutting.

2 What outcome does the other person expect from this situation?

Most managers are serving clients of some sort. Their client may be their boss, a colleague or an external partner. One way or the other, managers are supporting other people's agendas. Understanding what the other person wants is a very simple way of clarifying what the desired outcome of any situation is. Achieving clarity on this question enables the manager to:

● simplify and focus on the task in hand – the extraneous work quickly disappears

● predict and pre-empt problems and questions

● deliver appropriate outcomes to the other person.

Look back at the two examples (on the previous page). In each case, the individuals concerned were able to understand what they needed to do by understanding what 'the other person' wanted:

● The project team became focused on the outcome for the client.

● The analyst's presentation was focused on building a simple message for the person who needed to see the presentation.

3 What are the minimum number of steps required to get there?

There are plenty of people who make things complicated. While some people cannot see the wood for the trees, others cannot even see the trees for all the branches, twigs and leaves. Effective managers have a knack of making things simple. Given the increasing time pressure on all managers, this is an essential skill to have. Discovering

> Effective managers have a knack of making things simple.

the minimum number of steps requires asking a few more questions:

- What is the desired outcome (again)?
- Are there any shortcuts: can you buy in a solution, get someone else to provide all or part of the solution; is there an authoriser who can shortcut the normal approval channels?
- Does the 80/20 rule apply here: can you achieve 80 per cent of the result with just 20 per cent of the effort by focusing on the few customers who count, or the critical analysis that really will decide the issue, or by attacking the two big cost sinks that are causing the most problems?
- What are the critical dependencies? Normally, there is a logical order to events: billing comes after shipping comes after manufacturing comes after selling. Establishing this logical order breaks even the most daunting problem down into bite-sized chunks that people can manage.

4 What are the consequences of this course of action?

This question is about predicting risks, problems, unintended consequences and uncomfortable questions. If you can predict problems, you can pre-empt them. This is also the stage at which you may allow a little complexity to creep back into the course of action.

In theory, the shortest distance between two points is a straight line, except in non-Euclidean geometry. In practice, the fastest route often is not a straight line. When you are sailing against the wind, the fastest route between two points is a zigzag. Sailing straight into the wind gets you nowhere. This is an experience most managers understand after they have tried to sail against the political winds in their organisation.

The management mindset

1 **Start at the end**

Focus on the outcome and the results you want to achieve. Be relentless, stay focused.

2 **Work through others**

Do not try to be the lone hero. Management is about making things happen through other people. Learn to work through and with your peers, bosses and team members: influence, motivate, build trust and credibility.

3 **Drive to action**

Analysis shows you are smart; action shows you are effective. Do not look for the perfect answer: you will never find it. The perfect answer is the enemy of the practical answer. Find what works and do it.

4 **Take responsibility**

Do not blame others and focus on the past. Focus on the future, action and results. You are responsible for the outcome, for your career, for your conduct and for your feelings. Make the most of it.

5 **Be (selectively) unreasonable**

When you accept excuses you accept failure. Stretch yourself and your team. Be inflexible about goals but highly flexible about how you get there.

6 **Make a difference**

Performance is not measured in the volume of emails and meetings: it is measured in outcomes. Show you are relevant to the agenda of bosses two or three levels further up: work on a high-impact agenda.

7 **Be proactive**

Do not wait to be told. If you see an opportunity or a problem, use it as a chance to shine: take ownership. Embrace ambiguity and crises as chances to grow, learn and make a difference.

▶

8 Adapt

The rules of survival and success change by organisation and by level. Do not become a prisoner of past success. Continually learn, grow and adapt to the new rules of survival and success in your new context.

9 Work hard, work smart

There are no shortcuts or magic formulas. It is hard work. But work smart: manage time effectively and efficiently; focus on the right things; work through others and do not try to do it all yourself.

10 Act the part

Be a role model to others in what you do, how you look and how you behave. Act as you would like your peers to behave. Set yourself high standards, and then keep raising them.

The easiest way to work out the consequences of most actions is to understand who the major stakeholders are and how they will react: each stakeholder has a different perspective and will have different criteria and needs. The finance department will worry about affordability and payback; marketing will look at competitive reactions; sales will worry about price and positioning; HR will look at the staffing implications. Once you have a map of who is interested in what, then you can plot a zigzag through all the constituencies to make sure each one is able to satisfy their required needs.

2.2 Achieving results: performance and perceptions

Managers have to achieve results. Results are not always about delivering a profit: not everyone has P&L responsibility. Managers may be responsible for project outcomes, quality outcomes, costs, product design, development and delivery, and recruiting and training staff. There are endless possible results for which managers may be responsible. Ultimately, the test for a manager is to make sure they deliver those results. For better or for worse, many organisations do not look too closely at how results are achieved, unless there is immoral or illegal activity involved. Conversely, if a manager fails to deliver results, the manager fails. Results are better than excuses.

There are, essentially, five ways in which managers can achieve acceptable results:

1 Work harder.

2 Work smarter.

3 Fix the baseline.

4 Play the numbers game.

5 Manage for results.

1 Work harder

This is an unpalatable truth in the era of work–life balance, which is shorthand for a wish to work less. This is also the 24/7 era, when we are attached permanently to various electronic tags that constrain us as much as a prisoner's leg irons: there is no escape. Working harder, however, is not a lasting solution. Given the ambiguous nature of most managerial work, bosses do not know how much effort each manager is really putting in. If you achieve results, the assumption is that you can do more. So the reward for working harder is to get more work.

> The reward for working harder is to get more work.

You get less work only when you can no longer deliver or you complain loudly enough. Hard work is necessary, but it is not enough.

2 Work smarter

This is the desired outcome of results obsession: we find ways of doing things betterfastercheaper. Betterfastercheaper is the essence of capitalism. When a manager achieves betterfastercheaper, the ideal result is promotion. The more immediate consequence normally is the same as working harder: an increased workload rather than decreased working time. Like working harder, working smarter is necessary but not enough.

3 Fix the baseline

Beating a soft target is easier than beating a tough target. Many managers realise that it is better to negotiate hard for one month securing a soft target than it is to work hard for eleven months trying to beat a tough target. Even CEOs do this: watch the frequency with which a new CEO discovers a black hole in the organisation's finances that requires write-offs and adjustments to the corporate goals. Fixing the baseline does not enhance the prospects of the business, but it does enhance the prospects of your career.

4 Play the numbers game

There is an annual ritual in most organisations called 'meet year-end budget'. Experienced managers know that this is coming, and they know that, even if they are doing well, they are likely to be asked to deliver a little more in the last two months to make up for shortfalls elsewhere. This is where managers get creative. If they are doing well, they will hide spare budget for the inevitable year-end rainy day. If they are behind, they will use a combination of real actions on costs and whatever accounting smokescreens and mirrors can come to their support (see pages 80–81 for more detail). This may appear cynical, but it is part of the reality of management survival.

The first four approaches all depend on the manager doing things. The role of the manager is to make things happen through other people. This leads to the fifth managerial option, manage for results.

Unintended consequences of results obsession

Results focus has some unintended consequences. In the public sector, targets obsession leads to awkward outcomes, for instance:

- Schools are ranked on students' test results: they enrol pupils for the easiest subjects in order to increase pass rates. They try to pre-select students on ability so their overall results look good. Results improve, education does not.

- Hospitals are asked to reduce waiting times for operations: they use creative methods to move people off waiting lists and on to other sorts of lists; they require re-registration at frequent intervals so that people disappear off the list when they fail to re-register.

- Government needs to spend but also to meet its debt targets: it moves both spending and borrowing off its records by letting the private sector undertake major infrastructure projects (relating to hospitals, railways, etc.). If the private sector tried the same techniques, the regulators probably would start calling.

The private sector is not much better, for instance:

- The first edition of this book before the financial crash noted that: 'Banks reward loan officers on the volume of loans they make. Lending money to people is easy: getting it back is harder. By the time the bad debts mount up, the loan officers have received their bonus and moved on.' The crash was inevitable. Another will happen because nothing has changed. Traders are rewarded for taking huge risks, but their downside is limited if they lose.

- Train companies and airlines extend the published flying time on routes (London to Paris is 20 minutes slower than 30 years ago), which allows them to claim that more of their flights arrive on time.

- London Underground has reduced service frequency on the Circle Line to 'improve customer satisfaction'. This means that it can meet its published, but reduced, targets for the service being available. Ultimately, if it runs just one train an hour, it can achieve near 100 per cent service compliance and 100 per cent customer dissatisfaction.

5 Manage for results

Managers make things happen through other people. There is a huge difference between doing (working harder and smarter) versus managing (enabling other people to work harder and smarter). Managers who try to do it all themselves are not really managing and, in the long run, are condemned to fail. Management is a team sport.

As a manager, you have to make the crucial leap from 'how?' to 'who?'. As a team member, when you are assigned a task you may think, 'How do I do this?' As a manager, your reaction should be, 'Who can do this or help me do it?' No matter how creative you are in answering the 'how' question, there is a limit to what you can achieve. As soon as you start asking 'who', you are not constrained by the limits of your personal time, effort and insight. You start to unleash the efforts of the team and your colleagues.

You can manage for results only if you focus on the essence of management: making things happen through other people. You need to have the right people tackling the right challenges the right way: the focus of this book is on how you can make things happen through other people.

2.3 Making decisions: acquiring intuition fast

Decision-making principles

Good managers often are referred to as being decisive. 'Being decisive' is one of those vague management terms like 'professional', 'effective' or 'charismatic' that is very difficult to pin down; no one can teach it and it is assumed that either you have it or you do not. We found that decisive managers typically show four specific behaviours:

1 **Bias for action over analysis**. Actions achieve results, analysis does not. Less analysis can often lead to a better solution because it forces discussion to focus on the big issues that make a big difference. Often, detail derails decision making.

2 **Prefer practical to perfect solutions**. Accept that the perfect solution does not exist. Find a solution that will work in practice, even if it is not perfect in theory. The perfect solution is the enemy of the good solution because the search for perfection leads to inaction. A good solution leads to action.

3 **Solve the problem with other people**. Use the collective knowledge, wisdom and experience of the organisation to gain insight. Use it to identify and avoid the major risks and pitfalls. But do not convert a problem-solving process into a political negotiation in which the solution is a fix designed to pacify everyone. The result will be the least offensive rather than the most effective solution.

4 **Take responsibility**. Where there are shared and unclear responsibilities, most organisations breathe a huge sigh of relief if you have the courage to step up and take responsibility. You become the person to follow. It is a defining moment that separates leaders from followers: most people will be very happy to follow you.

The behaviours described above are hallmarks of a decisive manager, at least on minor matters such as sorting out late deliveries, staffing problems and budget arguments. But these useful instincts often desert managers when they are faced with a major decision. As the scale of the problem escalates, the number of people involved in it grows and the rational and political risks increase. Suddenly, managers become very risk averse. The manager's nightmare is to be held accountable for a decision that went wrong. To avoid this fate, managers seek refuge behind formal processes, exhaustive analysis and widespread consultation to optimise the decision and, more importantly, diffuse responsibility. Even if the decision turns out to be wrong, everyone has been so involved in the process that they will find it difficult to pin the blame on one person. What should be a rational process (make a decision) becomes a political process (avoid blame for a potentially damaging solution).

The larger the decision, the more risk averse managers become.

In general, the pay-off from making a risky and correct decision is quite low. Your success may be derailed by other factors or claimed by other people and, probably, it will have a minimal impact on your overall pay and promotion prospects. But the consequences of making a risky but incorrect decision are huge: colleagues will make sure that the blame is pinned on you, and your reputation will suffer.

A risky exercise

You are offered the chance to win £1,000 on a toss of a coin (a 50/50 chance, in theory). How much would you pay to play this game?

Most people will offer much less than £500, which should be the mean average pay-out from the game, if it is played enough times. Fear of loss outweighs the prospect of gain. Of course, make the game for 10 pence, and most people will play happily for 5 pence: risk aversion increases with the scale of the possible loss.

Decision-making traps

Analysis over action

Analysis is safe, action is risky. But analysis often throws up more challenges and more problems, which require more analysis. Slowly, the problem-solving exercise takes on a life of its own. No one can see through the thicket of challenges and problems that the analysis is throwing up. Paralysis through analysis becomes an unwelcome reality.

Seeking perfection over practicality

Faced with small problems, shortcuts seem acceptable. But bigger problems deserve better solutions, and the biggest problems deserve perfect solutions. The perfect solution must also be the least risky solution. Except that, in the messy world of management, there is no perfect solution. Any solution tends to be a trade-off between two unacceptable alternatives. No good solution exists on paper: good solutions exist only in reality.

> In the messy world of management, there is no perfect solution.

Hiding behind other people

It is far better to be wrong collectively than it is to be wrong individually: no one wants to run the risk of being asked to don the corporate equivalent of the dunce's cap. In some organisations, it is better to be wrong collectively than right individually: being right against the grain is seen to be disruptive to the team. Whistle blowers normally are vilified, not praised. The search for collective responsibility is natural risk avoidance. Collective responsibility requires consensus, which rarely represents the best solution. The consensus solution represents the least unacceptable solution to each constituency: it is a political fix. The purpose of involving other people should not be to achieve a consensus; it should be to gain insight. Ultimately, one person needs to own both the problem and the solution. They should use other people to gain insight and to drive action, not to hide behind in case things go wrong later.

Shedding responsibility

Responsibility for large problems, and their solutions, is often shared among several departments. This can lead to an unseemly game of pass the blame: no one really wants to be associated with causing the problem. Analysis of the problem becomes bogged down in an autopsy about what went wrong, rather than what the solution should be.

Decision making in practice

There are many decision-making and problem-solving tools available to managers and these are covered later in the chapter. In practice, managers rarely use such formal tools. Instead, there are three questions they ask themselves, which normally yield a practical answer:

1 Is there a pattern I recognise here?

2 Who does this decision matter to, and why?

3 Does someone know the answer anyway?

1 Is there a pattern I recognise here?

Pattern recognition is what managers often refer to as intuition or experience. Unlike intuition, however, pattern recognition can be learned. Pattern recognition is, simply, a matter of observing what works and what does not work in different situations. If you recognise a familiar pattern, you will be able to predict what actions will work or fail. You will appear to have intuitive business sense.

Learning to recognise patterns

Advertising is a curious world where the creativity of advertisers has to meet the disciplines of the marketplace. Good advertising can transform a brand; poor advertising can kill it. Either way, it costs a fortune to make and to air. The challenge for clients, who pay the advertising agencies, is to know whether their spending is going to work.

Procter & Gamble (P&G), one of the world's largest advertisers, does not rely on intuition. It has built up huge experience and has learned patterns of success and failure. Young brand managers have to acquire this intuition, or pattern recognition, fast. Inside the major offices of P&G there is a dark room where the secrets of advertising intuition are learned. On appointment, the first thing a brand manager will do is to go into this room and acquire the knowledge. He or she will do this by reviewing tapes of all the advertising the brand has aired in, perhaps, the past 50 years. Watching 50 years of Daz advertising is like watching a social history of Britain. And for each piece of advertising, there are key statistics to show how well it fared.

After a few hours of watching such advertising, even the rawest marketing manager acquires an uncanny ability to look at 30 seconds of advertising and to predict how well it scored and performed. This is intuition acquisition at speed. It cuts through theory and shows what works in practice.

Pattern recognition comes into play when the manager realises that he or she is going to be responsible for making a decision. If it is a familiar pattern, it is normally an easy decision (see the box above for a typical example).

Effective managers observe and learn from everyday situations to build up their knowledge of what does and does not work in their own organisation. We may not have the luxury of reviewing 50 years of people managing conflicts, negotiating, influencing people or problem solving, but good observation builds our skills, helps our pattern recognition and helps us appear to have excellent business sense and intuition.

Pattern recognition can be acquired and learned in a range of decision-making conditions:

- **Competitive reactions**. Long-established competitors know how one another will react, without the need for collusion, which would break anti-trust laws. In many markets, there is a price leader from whom all competitors take their cues. If the leader raises prices, everyone else follows. If there is a temporary price reduction for a promotion, competitors ignore it. If the price reduction is permanent, competitors follow. This makes pricing decisions across companies very simple: it is called follow my leader.

- **Buying decisions**. Philip Green is a billionaire retail entrepreneur who owns several fashion chains in the UK. When he looks at a rack of clothing, he is reputed to be able to cost each item accurately and to establish its proper retail price at a glance. Any buyer who is perceived to have overpaid for any line items is likely to have an uncomfortable discussion with the boss. Green is able to do this because he has seen thousands of racks of clothing over several decades of retail experience. His expert judgement is based on piling up the experience. He can demonstrate intuitively good sense on buying matters because he has seen the purchasing patterns so many times before.

- **Managing people**, including bosses, is largely about pattern recognition. We have to learn quickly what turns people on and off in terms of working style, risk appetite, people versus task focus, process versus outcome focus and more. No pattern is the right pattern: from the manager's perspective, the point is to learn what works with different people.

If a decision fits into a familiar pattern, then most managers have the confidence to make it. The P&G brand manager will approve the development of a new campaign based on judgement, without recourse to expensive and time-consuming market research. Green can buy effectively because he recognises the patterns unique to his trade.

2 Who does this decision matter to, and why?

Decision making is as much about politics as it is about reason. Managers need solutions that lead to action: the perfect solution that is not acted upon is useless. Decisions lead to action only if people support them. This means that managers will ask 'who?' as much as 'what?'.

> Decision making is as much about politics as it is about reason.

There are, essentially, four possibilities here, each with a different outcome, in terms of decision making:

1   **The decision is most important to a team member**.
    If possible, back the team member. Coach them and
    encourage them to arrive at a decision. Do not let them
    become dependent on you for making all their decisions:
    they will not grow professionally and you will die under an
    avalanche of requests for decisions.

2   **The decision is important for one of your bosses**. If you
    understand his or her agenda, it should be clear what the
    preferred decision is: frame the problem and the solution, and
    sell it to the boss. If the choice is unclear, work through the
    issue with the boss.

3   **The decision is important to another colleague**. Long
    term, managers need alliances and supporters across an
    organisation, so talk to the colleague and find a mutually
    advantageous solution. Help them: win a friend.

4   **The decision is important to you and your agenda**. If the
    choice is obvious, decide. If it is not, get help (see below).

This is decision making that is free of any problem-solving skills.
The key skills are understanding the agendas of bosses, colleagues
and your team, and framing the decision to support those agendas. For this reason, many decisions emerge gradually over time.
A consensus slowly builds, small actions are taken, which favour
one choice over another, and, gradually, a preferred course of
action emerges. This fits with the apparently chaotic schedule of
many managers: lots of small interactions over the day help them
understand one another's agendas, sell an agenda, gather information and migrate slowly towards a series of decisions.

3 Does someone know the answer anyway?

Management is a team sport. No single manager is expected to know
all the answers, but they may be expected to find all the answers.

For more complex decisions, no one knows the answer. But
many different individuals in finance, marketing, operations, IT,

sales and HR will hold part of the answer. They each hold one piece of the jigsaw and the job of the manager is to put the pieces together. This is both an intellectual process (discovering the best answer) and a political process (building a coalition in support of the emerging answer). This can take time. It may require several iterations before consensus can emerge and all the different agendas can be aligned.

In Japan, this consensus-based decision making is called *nemawashi*. The idea is to build agreement to the decision before the decision-making meeting. Carry out the initial conversations in private. This is critical. As soon as anyone has taken a position in public, they will feel the need to defend it at all costs, rather than lose face by changing their position. In private, you can have much more open and flexible conversations: real issues can be discussed, agendas can be aligned and commitment can be built. The more you listen, the more you will understand the politics of the decision and the views of different stakeholders. You will gain more insight into the nature of the decision: you will understand better what the real challenge is, what the different options are and the consequences of each option. The more you listen, the more likely it is that a consensus will emerge around one preferred solution.

How to influence decisions

1 Anchor the debate on your terms

   Strike early; set the terms of the debate around your agenda.

2 Build your coalition

   Manage disagreements in private; let people change their view without loss of face; publicise any agreements widely to build a bandwagon of support. Find powerful sponsors to endorse your position.

3 **Build incremental agreement**

Do not scare people by asking for everything at once. Ask individuals to back the one part of your idea where they have relevant expertise (finance, health and safety, etc.).

4 **Size the prize**

Build a clear, logical case that shows the benefits of your proposed course of action; quantify the benefits and have them endorsed appropriately.

5 **Frame the decision favourably**

Align your agenda with the corporate agenda; frame your idea in the right language and style for each person; be relentlessly positive.

6 **Restrict choice**

Do not give too many options: it will tend to confuse. Offer two or three choices at most.

7 **Work risk and loss aversion to your favour**

Show that alternatives to your idea are even riskier.

8 **Put idleness to work**

Make it easy for people to agree; remove any logistical or administrative hurdles for them.

9 **Be persistent**

Repetition works. What works? Repetition. Repetition works. The harder you practise, the luckier you get. Never give up.

10 **Adjust to each individual**

See the world through their eyes; respect their needs in terms of substance, style and format; build common cause; align your agendas.

The final decision-making meeting still has relevance, but it is not about making a decision. It is about confirming in public to all the stakeholders that there really is consensus and agreement.

It builds confidence and legitimises the decision that has been made already in private.

2.4 Solving problems: prisons and frameworks – and tools

Problem solving sometimes is thought to be the preserve of people who are brains on sticks. In reality, brains on sticks are precisely the wrong sort of people for solving most management problems: clever people search fruitlessly for the non-existent perfect solution so they achieve nothing. A workable solution is preferable to the perfect solution because it leads to action. The perfect solution is the enemy of the practical solution.

Three principles lie behind effective problem solving:

1   Know your problem.

2   Focus on causes, not symptoms.

3   Prioritise the problems.

> Smart managers think they know all the answers. Really smart managers know the right questions.

Smart managers think they know all the answers. Really smart managers know the right questions. The best answer to the wrong question is useless. The purpose of this section is to help you identify the right problem, ask the right questions and arrive at a practical solution.

1 Know your problem

All students are given strict briefing before sitting any exam: 'Make sure you answer the question.' This is remarkably obvious advice, which is ignored remarkably often – with catastrophic consequences. The same advice needs to be given to all managers: 'Make sure you answer the question.' At least with school exams, the question is clear. In business, no one hands out an exam paper: you are expected to know what the exam question is without being told.

At junior levels of management, the exam questions are often pretty clear. They tend to be expressed as simple performance goals: sell more product, trade more profitably, bill more personal time. As managers continue their careers, clarity reduces and ambiguity increases. The goal may be clear (make your profit target) but the means to the end are not. It pays to fight the right battles the right way to achieve the overall goal. You have to know which the right battles are.

Know your problem

This was my big break. I got to present to the CEO. I gave what I thought was a brilliant presentation. At the end of it, the CEO coughed quietly and seemed to confirm my judgement of my own talents.

'That was a very impressive presentation,' he said. 'I only have one question...'

I was ready for any question. I had 200 back-up pages of detailed analysis. This was my chance to shine.

'What, precisely, was the problem you were solving?' he asked.

That was the one question I was not ready for. I quickly vanished into a puff of my own vanity and confusion.

2 Focus on causes, not symptoms

No one would think of trying to cure chicken pox by using spot remover. But such confusion over symptoms and causes happens regularly in business. Many cost-cutting programmes fall into this trap. The CEO looks strong and effective announcing some target job cuts or cost savings. In highly macho form the message was conveyed to the CEO's management team as: 'Give me 20 per cent cost reduction and 20 per cent head count in 12 months, or you will be part of the 20 per cent. No excuses.'

Over 15 per cent was delivered and some top executives were fired. It took years for the business to recover from the mindless cost cutting of marketing (loss of market position and revenues), of R&D (loss of new product flow) and of talent (loss of morale).

Cost problems are always a symptom of something else, such as:

- inadequate revenues, which in turn may be a product problem, marketing and sales problem, distribution problem
- wrong product and customer mix, which are expensive to serve and do not pay enough to justify the cost
- ineffective processes and inefficient working practices.

The business goes in dramatically different directions if you choose to focus on increasing revenues, changing the product and customer mix or improving processes and working practices. Simple head count reduction will not achieve any of these positive outcomes.

> Understanding the causes of good or poor performance is as important as measuring the outcome.

On a smaller scale, many HR practices deal with symptoms, not causes. Performance-based appraisal and promotion systems sound highly dynamic. But they focus on symptoms (how well did the person do?) versus causes. Understanding the causes of good or poor performance is at least as important as measuring the outcome:

- Why did they do well or poorly?
- What skills need to grow to raise performance?
- What assignments will best suit this person in future?
- Are they building the right skills and experiences for their career and promotion prospects?
- How can performance be improved?

The skills-based approach to appraisal results in a better appraisal discussion. The good/bad performance appraisal can be confrontational and not very actionable. Many managers shy away from giving bad news, which helps no one.

Anyone can spot a symptom of a problem. It does not take a genius to see that profits are not high enough. The mark of a good manager is one who can go beyond symptoms and unearth the root causes of the problem. There are no easy shortcuts available. But there is one simple principle – keep on asking one question: 'Why?'

3 Prioritise the problems

Management is never short of problems and challenges. There are not enough hours in the day to solve them all. So managers have to be selective. Three simple questions help identify which problems are worth addressing:

1 **Is it important?** Does this problem make a significant difference to achieving your overall goals? Put another way, if this problem is not resolved, will it have a serious adverse effect? Is there a simple stop-gap solution, which will prevent things getting worse while you concentrate on other problems?

2 **Is it urgent?** Do today what you have to do today. Will the problem be worse tomorrow than it is today, and does it matter? If it does, act now. Can you buy time? Problems do not always become worse: time has a habit of throwing up more information, more opportunities and more potential solutions. It can also heal emotional upsets.

3 **Is it actionable?** One of the dubious joys of management is to have to live with problems that you can do little or nothing about. You may be at the mercy of strategic challenges and decisions, IT projects going awry or competitive pressures forcing sudden and unexpected demands on you. Under these circumstances, the best thing to do is nothing. Focus on what you can control, not on what you cannot control.

Problem-solving tools

Most managers solve most problems intuitively. It is rare that managers sit down and do a formal problem analysis. But it helps to have a few tools and techniques at hand. You do not need to get pen and paper out every time you want to use them. It is enough to have the frameworks in your mind, and then you can use them to check and challenge your own thinking.

Here, we cover six classic problem-solving aids:

1 Cost–benefit analysis.

2 SWOT analysis.

3 Field force analysis.

4 Multifactor/trade-off/grid analysis.

5 Fishbone/mind maps.

6 Creative problem solving.

No single way is the best way. They all have value in different contexts. The key is to pick the right approach for the right context.

Typical assumptions for each approach are:

1 **Cost–benefit analysis**. Assumes a well-defined problem and solution that needs to be evaluated financially for formal approval.

2 **SWOT analysis**. Assumes a highly ambiguous, often strategic, challenge that needs further structuring.

3 **Field force analysis**. Assumes a choice is to be made between two courses of action including non-financial and qualitative criteria.

4 **Multifactor/trade-off/grid analysis**. Assumes a choice between multiple competing options with multiple criteria of varying importance.

5 **Fishbone/mind maps**. Assumes that there is a problem where the root causes need to be identified and broken down into bite-sized chunks.

6 **Creative problem solving**. Assumes a highly complex problem to which there is no known answer and for which an original approach is required.

1 Cost–benefit analysis

This is the staple of all good management decision making. When it is not used, disaster often ensues. The disciplines of cost–benefit analysis are abused most commonly on IT system changes, which are sold in on the basis of being strategic. When IT managers say strategic they often mean expensive.

A strong cost–benefit analysis is highly compelling. It forces management to take a proposal seriously: no executive wants to turn down a credible proposal that is financially attractive. The key here is credibility. It is not enough to produce a financially attractive proposal. It has to be credible. There are three elements to making the proposal credible:

1 Strong, logical reasoning.

2 Validation of the numbers by the finance department: if it does not support the calculations, then you are finished. Involve finance early, get its advice and buy-in. Make sure you produce numbers to a format that finance recognises and can approve.

3 Operational credibility. Venture capitalists look beyond the numbers to the people who are behind the numbers. They back people as much as they back ideas. Executives do the same. It pays to find highly credible supporters and backers for your proposal.

Each organisation will have its own way of looking at financial benefits. The most common are:

● payback period

● ROI (return on investment)

● NPV (net present value).

Of these three, payback is the simplest, but NPV is the most rigorous and is relatively easy. ROI is included only because it is widely used: in its simple form it is misleading and in its more refined form it is very complicated.

Payback period

How long will it take me to recoup my investment? One bank has a three-year payback period for staff redundancies. If it costs £100,000 to fire someone who costs the bank £50,000 a year including benefits, then the payback period is two years and it passes the three-year test, provided no replacement is hired.

ROI: return on investment

This is where things get sticky. There are many different ways of calculating ROI. Each expert will start climbing the wall and spitting blood if you do not use their pet method. So the advice is to work with your finance department and discover which rules it plays to. Enlist its support and, preferably, get it to do the calculation for you. The problems start with knowing what the required rate of return should be. There are long and tedious debates about this, which involve discussion of forecast and historic equity risk premiums, and one- versus five-year betas, and much

Work with your finance department and discover which rules it plays to.

more. We will avoid that debate for now. For most managers, the required ROI is mandated from above. It may vary according to the risk of the project: a cost-savings programme may have a required return of 10 per cent; expansion into a new market may have a required return of 15 per cent to adjust for the risk of the project. To do this analysis you need to know the cost of the investment and the net benefits it will produce over its lifetime, together with whatever rate of return you are required to achieve. A simple worked example, looking at the cost of installing AVR (automatic voice response) in a call centre to replace humans, follows.

Worked example (1)

The cost of the AVR machine is £1,000 today. It will cost £100 a year to maintain, but it will save £500 of labour, so the net annual benefit is £400. At the end of four years, it will be given away to charity: it will have no resale value.

The ROI calculation now looks like this:

(a) Required return: 15 per cent

(b) Year	0	1	2	3	4	Total
(c) Investment (£)	−1,000					−1,000
(d) Net benefit (£)		400	400	400	400	+1,600

The simplest form of ROI is as follows: ((Total benefits − total costs)/total costs) $\times$ (100/number of years). In this case, the calculation would be:

$$ROI = ((1,600 - 1,000)/1,000) \times 100/4 = 15\%$$

This shows that this investment just meets the corporate goal of 15 per cent ROI.

This simple form of ROI is misleading. It assumes that a pound today is worth as much as a pound in four years' time: the next section shows this is untrue. The alternative to this form of ROI allows for the different value of a pound over time. It is called IRR (internal rate of return) and is, effectively, the ROI on an investment, which results in an NPV of zero. This requires first understanding NPV, which is useful.

The most practical solution is to work with whatever rules your finance department has in place. The rules may be wrong and misleading, but, if that is how decisions are made, then it makes sense to work to them.

NPV: net present value

This is, perhaps, the most orthodox and reliable form of cost–benefit analysis.

The one key concept here is the discount rate. This is a way of saying that a pound today is worth more than a pound tomorrow: I can invest today's pound and make it worth £1.10 this time next year. And your promise of a pound next year is much more risky than your offer of a pound right now. Because of risk, I will take less than one pound (perhaps even 70 pence) right now instead of a promise of a pound later. The discount rate adjusts for the time and risk effects of accepting a pound later instead of a pound now.

A 15 per cent discount rate implies that a pound now is worth as much as a promise of £1.15 next year, £1.32 the year after and about £2 in five years' time. To put it the other way round: if I am promised £2 in five years' time, that is worth about £1 to me today.

I apply a discount factor of 0.5 to the promise of a pound in five years' time.

Worked example (2)

NPV of AVR machine

(a) Required return: 15 per cent

(b) Year	0	1	2	3	4	Total
(c) Discount factor	1	0.87	0.76	0.66	0.57	
(d) Investment (£)	−1,000					
(e) Cost savings (£)		400	400	400	400	
(f) Discounted cost/benefit:	−1,000	348	302	263	229	+142

This analysis also shows that the AVR is a worthwhile investment. But it is a very limited calculation because:

- it does not factor in major sensitivities and uncertainties (see below)
- it ignores second-order effects (disgruntled customers left hanging on the phone, and possibly switching supplier)
- it ignores alternatives (outsourcing or offshoring the call centre, upgrading the call centre to make it revenue generating through cross selling, segmenting the customers so that high-profit customers still get personal service, etc.).

Sensitivity analysis

This gets us into the land of what if, for which spreadsheets are a saviour. What if calculations allow us to test our major assumptions. For instance, in the NPV example above, the AVR project becomes unattractive (it achieves a negative NPV) if:

- the required return is raised to 20 per cent
- the AVR needs to be replaced after three years, not four
- the net cost savings turn out to be £300 per year, not £400
- the AVR kit costs £1,200.

Managers quickly learn how to manipulate assumptions to ensure the right answer appears in the bottom right-hand corner of the spreadsheet.

In the most sophisticated world, different outcomes can be assigned different probabilities and a weighted NPV can be derived. Probability analysis is important in some industries: the profitability of financial leasing of computers depends heavily on resale values and likely depreciation rates; exploration for oil depends heavily on probabilities. But, for most management decisions, decision making is much simpler. If a project only just scrapes past a cost–benefit analysis, it probably is not worth it: you know the numbers will have been fixed to pass the test and

> **If a project is worthwhile, it sails past any cost–benefit analysis.**

that reality is unlikely to be as rosy as the forecast. If a project is worthwhile, it sails past any cost–benefit analysis with ease. If it under-delivers against forecast, it may still beat the required return for the organisation as a whole.

2 SWOT analysis

Not all problems succumb immediately to a cost–benefit analysis. Cost–benefit analysis implies a degree of certainty about outcomes. Managers know that the only true certainty is uncertainty. Putting some structure into ambiguous and uncertain situations helps decision making and problem solving. Perhaps the simplest way of structuring unstructured problems is a SWOT analysis. SWOT stands for:

Strengths

Weaknesses

Opportunities

Threats

SWOT is a simple way of looking at strategic challenges. For instance, should Techmanics (a fictitious company) expand into China?

Strengths: Techmanics has some great technology and wonderful products that no one else can fully match. Strong R&D will keep us ahead of competition.

Weaknesses: no Chinese distribution, no Chinese staff who can understand the market.

Opportunities: vast and growing market, especially in the luxury and gadget segment where Techmanics is focused. The high end of the market is highly profitable.

Threats: no intellectual property protection – Techmanics' products may be ripped off. Death Star Ventures may enter China before we do and condemn us to being also-rans.

This highly simplified SWOT analysis shows:

- the value of structuring a difficult challenge: it gives a framework for further discussion
- the value of exploring alternative perspectives: it looks at the costs and opportunities of expanding and *not* expanding into China, and at possible competitive reactions
- the need to frame the issue before embarking on a detailed cost–benefit analysis.

3 Field force analysis

Field force analysis is a very fancy way of writing down the pros and cons, or the benefits and concerns of a specific decision. It is best used to evaluate a specific course of action where there are multiple, qualitative factors which affect the outcome. For instance, one company had a discussion about whether to introduce a floor cleaner based on a successful bathroom surface cleaner which already existed.

For the new product	Against the new product
Exploits an existing, trusted brand name	Might damage the existing brand
Uses spare factory capacity	Manufacturing complexity: changeovers
Attacks competitor's profit sanctuary	Might lead to an expensive marketing war
Floor cleaners are a huge market	Expensive, risky to build market share
Our product is superior to competition	Competitor's products are well established
Our market tests went well	National conditions not the same as the test market

This simple analysis helps frame and focus the discussion. The 'Against' column becomes a risk and issue register. Standard problem-solving and brainstorming methods can be used to help resolve each of the risks and issues identified.

4 Multifactor/trade-off/grid analysis

This family of problem-solving analyses is a good way of making a choice between multiple, hard-to-compare options. The real value of this approach is that it forces people to think about the criteria they are using to make a decision. It forces them to be explicit about how important one criterion is relative to another. This cuts through many rambling debates where managers are arguing for different choices and are using compelling but competing arguments. All the arguments cancel each other out and result in a tense stalemate. This approach prevents the stalemate and leads to a much more productive discussion.

It has six simple steps:

1 List the criteria for making the decision.

2 Score each criterion for how important it is.

3 List your options.

4 Score each option against each criterion.

5 Adjust the raw scores for the weightings you gave in step 2.

6 Add the scores up and, hopefully, come to an agreed outcome: if not, at least you will know why and, where you disagree, you can have a more focused discussion.

The following example looks at the choice of a new office.

Choosing a new office

Start with the unweighted scores out of ten.

	Property			
Criterion	1	2	3	4
Ease of access for staff	9	3	6	7
Ease of access for customers	4	6	7	6
Cost	2	9	7	5
Length of lease	4	9	2	7
Layout of office	9	4	6	3
Prestige of building and address	9	2	6	4
Total	37	33	34	32

The first cut seems to show that property 1 is a clear winner. At this point, the CEO steps in and points out that, just as all executives are not equal, so all criteria are not equal. The CEO assigns weightings to the criteria with the following results, where the unweighted scores simply have been multiplied by the weightings assigned by the CEO:

	Property			
Criterion (and CEO's weighting)	1	2	3	4
Ease of access for staff (2)	18	6	12	14
Ease of access for customers (7)	28	42	49	42
Cost (10)	20	90	70	50
Length of lease (6)	24	54	12	42
Layout of office (5)	45	20	30	15
Prestige of building and address (4)	36	8	24	16
Total	171	220	197	179

The CEO either is fundamentally mean or is a diligent steward of shareholders' money. Either way, costs dominate the weightings, so that property 1 falls from being first choice to last and property 2 becomes a clear winner, even though layout and access for staff look highly unattractive.

5 Fishbone/mind maps

This family of problem-solving techniques is another area that has been hijacked by experts. These techniques are useful for breaking down a big problem into bite-sized chunks. They are also a good way of discovering the root cause of a problem, as opposed to its symptoms. They are very visual exercises, which often are best done in small groups. The experts are very particular about making you use different colours for different parts of your diagram and can inflict an entire philosophy on your simple need to solve a problem.

For our purposes, we can keep it simple. A simplified example of a fishbone analysis is shown opposite.

The key steps are:

1 State the problem (which appears as the head of the fish in the fishbone).

2 Identify some of the major possible causes of the problem (the big bones of the fish).

3 Drill down in each major area and identify specific issues to address or investigate further (the small bones in the fish). You can drill down even further on any of these items, if necessary.

As a result of this brainstorming, you will have identified the major causes of the problem/symptom. If there is agreement about the root cause, move to action. Otherwise, you may need to do some more legwork to understand individual issues. Either way, you will have broken down a big and messy problem into manageable chunks, and you will have moved away from dealing with symptoms to dealing with root causes. These are two

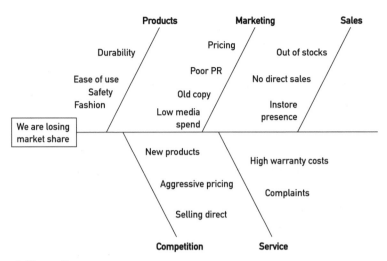

Fishbone diagram

valuable outcomes, especially if achieved in a group setting where you build buy-in and commitment to the way forward.

6 Creative problem solving

Not all problems can be solved by force of logic. The more interesting management challenges require a degree of creativity and invention. Asking managers to be creative will result in most of them breaking out in a cold sweat: creative workshops conjure up images of abysmal sessions where we all have to say what sort of tree/car/musician we would be if we were a tree/car/musician. Fortunately, there are some reliable ways of arriving at creative solutions without enduring the terminal embarrassment of a creativity workshop.

The simplest solution is to ask for help. You may not know the solution, but others may. Even if they do not have the total solution, they can provide insights, which may help

> The simplest solution is to ask for help.

you. There are plenty of exercises that demonstrate the power of the group to find a better solution than an individual can find. Desert, moon, space and island survival are all classic group dynamics exercises that prove the point. Type 'desert survival' into any search engine and you will find plenty of helpful and free examples on the web.

The more formal solution is to ask for help in a structured way, through a problem-solving exercise. Here is a straightforward way to conduct the exercise in a series of steps:

1   Agree who is the problem owner and what the problem is that you need to solve. Try to make the problem as specific and as focused as possible. Also, try to express it as an outcome. General and negative problems are difficult to solve, such as 'We are losing in the market.' Define the problem more closely and positively. 'How to increase retention rates among our most loyal customers' is going to lead to more actionable and positive solutions than the more general and negative version of the problem statement.

2   Outline the problem to a small group of people who between them have the knowledge, willingness and capability to provide insight and solutions. The ideal group has about four to seven people in it. Any fewer, and there are not enough to generate ideas and enthusiasm. Any more and it becomes chaotic.

3   Check for understanding of the problem statement, so that everyone is solving the same problem. Allow questions to check understanding, avoiding any evaluation of the problem.

4   Generate ideas, and lots of them. Volume is good. Do not allow any evaluation of ideas at this stage. Get people to build on each other's ideas. Get people to look at the problem from different angles (competitors, customers, channels, costs, products, service, etc.) to stimulate more ideas. One person records the ideas on a flipchart: this avoids too much duplication and lets contributors see that their ideas have been recognised so they do not feel the need to repeat themselves. Make things move fast: make people state only the headline of their idea. As with any good newspaper, the headline should encapsulate the whole story. This makes it easier to record.

5 Select a few ideas to work on in detail. You can permit an outbreak of democracy at this stage. Give each person three votes, using Chicago rules. Chicago rules mean that there are no rules: they can split their votes, sell their votes, steal votes or consolidate their votes. Do not get hung up on process. If two people had similar ideas, let them consolidate them into one: do not have a big debate, just let the owners of the two ideas decide if they want to merge. Normally, you will find that there is consensus around three to five workable ideas, and you will have done no evaluation of them so far.

6 Evaluate the most popular idea. Start by looking at why it is a good idea: evaluate its benefits. Managerial instinct is to look at problems first. The problem with problem focus is that it can kill good ideas. Once you understand why an idea is good, you can start to explore some of the concerns it raises. Express the concerns in an action-focused manner: 'How to fund the idea' leads to action, whereas 'That is far too expensive' leads to conflict. How you state the concern leads to radically different outcomes.

7 If the solution you are all most excited about has some significant concerns attached, work through each of those concerns using the same process, starting at step 1 again. You will find yourself breaking the problem down into ever more manageable bite-sized chunks that you can deal with.

Problem solving for managers

1 Find the right problem

The right answer to the wrong problem is wrong. Focus on causes, not symptoms. Understand why the problem has arisen.

▶

2 **Find the problem owner**

Find out who owns the problem and why it matters to them. They may know the answer already, so ask them. Establish how important and urgent it is and gauge your response accordingly.

3 **Use your experience**

You have expertise and experience in your role: use it. If you have seen this sort of problem before, you should know what to do. So do it.

4 **Ask**

If you are unsure what the best solution is, ask for advice. Your peers may have the answer, although they may all have different answers.

5 **Avoid the perfect solution**

The perfect answer is the enemy of the practical answer, because you will never find the perfect answer. Find what works and do that.

6 **Stay future focused**

Do not dwell on the past or try to apportion blame. Look to the future, look to action.

7 **Focus on benefits before concerns**

It is easier to spot risks than opportunities. But, if you focus on the risks of every solution, you will be paralysed by fear. Focus on the benefits first: if the benefits are big enough, then it is worth dealing with the risks.

8 **Build a coalition in support of your solution**

Asking for advice has the virtue of building consensus and paving the way for your solution to be put into action.

9 **Keep it simple**

Do not boil the ocean of facts and analysis. Use formal problem-solving techniques sparingly: they are an aid to thinking, not a substitute for thinking. The best solutions are discovered through action, not designed through analysis.

10   Drive to action

There is no such thing as a good idea that never happened. A solution is good only if it happens. A partial solution is often enough: you can then build on that and improve it.

2.5 Strategic thinking: floors, romantics and the classics

If you listen to business school professors, strategy is so sophisticated and complicated that only they can really understand it. To prove their point, they come up with all sorts of clever concepts, such as value innovation, strategic intent, core competences and co-creation. These are supported by matrices, grids and charts that give the appearance of analytical rigour.

Do not be deceived. Most strategic concepts are:

● selective rewriting of history of some successful companies
● better at describing the past than predicting the future
● based on a few simple truths.

Most corporate strategy is formulated the same way as most corporate budgets: last year's budget and strategy is the best predictor of next year's budget and strategy. Both will change, incrementally. But few companies actually change strategy significantly. The exceptions are famous, but exceptional. WPP, the world's largest advertising conglomerate, was formed out of a shell company that made shopping trolleys. Nokia, once the world's largest maker of mobile phones, had its origins in rubber (largest shoe factory in Europe), plastics (floor coverings) and forestry products.

> Last year's budget and strategy is the best predictor of next year's budget and strategy.

Because most businesses do not change strategy fundamentally, the demand for deep strategic thinking from managers is not high. Nevertheless, it helps to understand strategic thinking, so:

1   Understand the strategic relevance of your own activities.

2   Know how to think strategically.

3   Play the strategy game.

4   Understand the nature of strategy.

If you can do these four things, you are well prepared for the executive suite.

1 Understand the strategic relevance of your own activities

I started to doubt the use of the word strategy when the office manager started talking about strategic deployment of office space. I retired to the canteen to consider how I might strategically deploy my Brussels sprouts. As ever, the office manager was right and I was left to eat cold Brussels sprouts.

The office manager was answering the one strategic question that all managers have to be able to answer: 'How can my actions and decisions support the goals of the organisation?' At the risk of stating the obvious, this requires more than simply understanding the goals you have been set in your annual plan: it requires understanding the goals of the senior leadership team. Many managers fail this obvious test: they are so consumed with meeting their immediate goals that they forget to think about the broader context in which they are operating.

The office manager had a strategic challenge all of his own. As we walked round the office we could see lots of consultants working in individual glass fish bowls: these were meant to combine privacy with open communication. In practice, the walls stopped communication and the glass prevented privacy. The manager had heard the CEO talk about the need for teamwork, transparency and focus on clients: that meant working at the client site, not in our cosy offices. The manager thought it through, and came up with a radically new design.

Out went all the mini-palaces that were also known as partners' offices. Instead, we were invited to share a common partners' room: we were being asked to walk the talk on teamwork. Quite a few partners exploded with indignant rage: they were the idle ones who would be most exposed in a common office. Next step were the consultants. Out went their goldfish bowls and their desks. In came rows of hot desks. There were not enough to go round, so consultants suddenly found it more congenial to work at the client site. In came lots of small meeting places so that teams could meet and work together.

The office manager had grasped the nature of strategy: he had understood the needs of the organisation and taken action to support them. He had no need to understand grand corporate strategy, or to talk the language of core competences. They were irrelevant. Managers do not need to be great strategists to think and act strategically: they need to understand the real needs of the organisation and to support those needs in their areas.

A simple test for strategic activity is this: will these actions get noticed at executive committee level? If they are relevant at that level, you are probably acting on matters that have strategic relevance. If not, you may still be making a useful but less visible contribution.

2 Know how to think strategically

The best strategic thinking is very simple: clever people make things complicated; really clever people make things simple.

> The best strategic thinking is very simple: clever people make things complicated; really clever people make things simple.

Many of the most successful organisations have very simple strategies:

- easyJet and Southwest Airlines: low-cost flying.
- Dell: sell direct and make to order.
- FedEx: overnight delivery, guaranteed.

Although they are very simple strategies, they are competitively devastating. Let us look at each in more detail to see why:

- **easyJet and Southwest Airlines: low-cost flying**. By starting with a zero cost base, and avoiding all the frills and complexity of full-service airlines, they achieved cost per mile and fares, which the full-service airlines cannot reach with their legacy costs and infrastructure. They created clear competitive distance against the incumbents.

- **Dell: sell direct and make to order**. This eliminated all the sales forecasting problems, unsold stocks, cash-flow crises and fire sales that dogged the traditional model of selling through resellers. Incumbents felt unable to abandon their loyal resellers and were stuck.

- **FedEx: overnight delivery, guaranteed**. No one else did it at the time. Creating the nationwide infrastructure and building volume and scale fast made it hard for anyone to follow.

Now consider how much these strategies have changed over the past 20 years. Each organisation essentially has the same strategic formula as 20 years ago. Great strategies rarely change.

3 Play the strategy game

If you ever apply to join a strategy consulting firm, you will get a chance to play the strategy game, also known as the case method interview. It is worth practising this game: it gives insight into the prospects of your employer and enables you to hold your own in discussions with senior executives.

The ostensible purpose of the game is to find an answer to some imponderable business question, such as: 'Should MegaBucks expand its product range from photography to other imaging products like copiers?' The real purpose of the game is to show that you can think in a structured and strategic manner: the actual answer is unimportant. Cynics might say that it is the essence of strategy consulting: show you are smart and do not worry too much about the answer.

> To succeed, you do not need to know the right answer. You need to know the right questions.

To succeed, you do not need to know the right answer. You need to know the right questions. An effective strategy discussion will look at the issue from a series of different angles:

- **What capabilities do we have?** This gets at the core competence arguments of Hamel and Prahalad (management thinkers and academics). Imaging and photographic technology are close to each other, as Canon discovered by bridging both markets.

- **What are the market prospects?** Is it growing? Is it profitable? What are the pricing trends? Critically, you need to look at individual segments of the market. Which ones are underserved? What needs are unmet? Canon identified that the old central copying function, focused on high volume, did not meet the needs of secretaries who needed just one or two quick copies locally. There was an unmet need for quick, cheap and average-quality copies. High speed was not important.

- **What does the competition look like?** Again, look for underserved market segments. Xerox was huge and looked unbeatable. But it had no product for distributed/local copying across the office.

- **What are the economics of the market from a customer perspective?** Instead of being tied into long leases for big copiers, secretaries would be happy to buy cheap local copiers.

- **What are the economics from the manufacturer's perspective?** The big money is in the replacement toner. This means the key is to get the copier on to the secretary's desk, if necessary at a loss, and then make money on the supplies. This then implies that the product must be simple to maintain and resupply, without the need for a technician. This in turn leads to a distribution model that is more mass market, accessed via resellers rather than through the traditional model of B2B salesmen working on commission.

As you go through the game, you should keep in mind a checklist of questions and perspectives you need to cover:

- capabilities of the firm and its rivals
- market prospects, by segment – size, growth, profitability and cyclicality
- customer needs, by segment – remember product, price, positioning questions
- competitive position, by segment. What is our value proposition? Do we have any sustainable advantage, barriers to entry?
- economics, relative to competition, the customer and us. What are the effects of scale across the value chain? What is the value chain?

Keep asking these questions until you find convincing answers. Quite often, you will find that just one critical insight develops out of all the questions. In the exotic world of wet cement supply, the economics of distribution favour the creation of a series of local monopolies. It takes some questioning to get to that simple outcome. Asking the set questions will help you quickly identify why Microsoft is highly profitable, whereas airlines are, at best, cyclical in terms of profitability.

4 Understand the nature of strategy

It helps to know the language of strategy. Strategy is spoken in two very different languages: the classical and the postmodern.

Classical strategy

Classical strategy is a world of cause and effect. It is a search for the business equivalent of Newton's laws: 'If **x** happens, then **y** is the result.' It is strategy in the true tradition of the Enlightenment: finding universal rules to apply to all situations. The godfathers of this world are Michael Porter (Five Forces analysis) and the Boston Consulting Group (responsible for matrix mania). The good news is that these formulae shed light, and provide some insight, into complex situations.

The bad news about formulaic strategy is that it is extremely dangerous. If everyone uses the same tools and the same analyses, they come up with the same answers. This leads to the lemming syndrome: '10,000 lemmings cannot be wrong, so I will jump off a cliff as well...' The dotcom bomb was a classic lemming moment.

UK telcos all did the same analysis and bid £22.4 billion for 3G licences: it is unlikely that they will ever get that money back. When many of the world's banks decided to chase profits by lending to the sub-prime markets, creating complex derivatives and increasing their capital leverage, they were, possibly, smart individual decisions. Collectively, they built a house of cards that fell down and led to global recession. Following the herd can be very dangerous.

Postmodern strategy

This is the language of a group of professors who all learned their trade from C.K. Prahalad (core competence, strategic intent). His acolytes include Gary Hamel, Chan Kim (value innovation) and Venkat Ramaswamy (co-creation). They are rebels against classical orthodoxy. For them, strategy is a process of discovery in which you create the future, rather than react to the present by analysing the past. This is a process-driven view of strategy much more than an analytical view of strategy. It does not pretend to have all the answers: it challenges organisations to discover and create answers for themselves.

The good news about this approach is that it leads to much more creative outcomes and engages the organisation more deeply. The bad news is that often it is not practical. It seeks radical strategic change, but most large organisations either do not need radical redirection, or are not capable of achieving it.

On balance, the classical approach to strategy suits established firms best. New entrants and start-ups use the postmodern approach, but are too small to realise that they are doing so.

Financial skills

Financial numeracy is a core skill for all managers. Unfortunately, financial skills are shrouded in unnecessary mystery. The high priests of accounting and finance cloak their art in terminology and techniques that are designed to scare off most managers. They are like medieval craft guilds who jealously protected their trade from all outsiders. Some areas of finance and accounting are genuinely complicated: understanding regulatory capital requirements for banks internationally is not the sort of area the average manager needs or wants to understand. It is now clear that not even bankers or their regulators understood this either. But the core financial and accounting skills should be core skills for all managers.

These skills are not purely intellectual skills. Most financial management skills are deeply political, because they involve allocation of resources, setting of targets, expectations and priorities. Inevitably, this goes to the heart of competitive strategy: how each department and each manager competes against the others to secure the right resources, expectations and targets. Formal financial tools are simply the weapons of choice for managers in these political and competitive battles. Only the most naive managers accept financial management as an objective, logical and rational exercise in which right and wrong answers can be discovered intellectually. The right financial solution is the one that best helps each manager to achieve their optimum goals.

The core financial skills required of all managers are explored in the following sections:

Setting budgets

Managing budgets

Managing costs

Surviving spreadsheets

Knowing numbers

These are the main financial and political battlegrounds for managers. Within each of these battlegrounds there are accepted weapons, or analytical tools, that managers can use to achieve their goals. The nature of these weapons differs slightly by organisation. In any event, it is worth learning how to use these weapons to best advantage. Most traditional financial textbooks focus on finding the right answer and the right number. Managers do not use numbers in an intellectual pursuit of the ideal answer. Managers use numbers the same way lawyers use facts: selectively to support their case, not to illuminate the truth.

> Managers use numbers the same way lawyers use facts: selectively to support their case, not to illuminate the truth.

2.6 Setting budgets: the politics of performance

A budget is a contract between two levels of management: 'We agree to achieve the following in return for this much money.' As with all contracts, this is not a rational and objective exercise. It is a negotiation between the supplier of services (the less senior manager) and the buyer with the money (the more senior manager). Unlike most negotiations, both the buyer and the seller in budget negotiations have roughly similar levels of information; they know each other's tactics and they know each other's styles. So the negotiation can become very intense.

Most budget negotiations have two major elements: anchoring and adjustments.

Anchoring the budget discussion

The best predictor of next year's budget is this year's budget. This year's budget is the anchor around which next year's budget will be negotiated. In many organisations, this is so well established that managers will fight hard to spend this year's budget fully and to not over-achieve budget this year: underspending or over-achieving simply leads to the budget anchor being reset. Next year's budget becomes much harder to achieve if you do too well this year (see the boxed example on the next page). Such budget setting clearly is dysfunctional: it discourages performance improvement.

To effect real change, the anchor needs to be reset at a very different point from today. Anchoring needs to be achieved as early as possible, so that the debate is framed the right way. If the debate is framed around 'How far do we increase or decrease last year's budget?', only minor change will emerge. If the debate is anchored around 'Can we double our volume with just a 70 per cent increase in budget?', you have a radically different discussion. Anchoring determines the level of ambition for the organisation.

Anchoring needs to take place as part of the strategic planning process, which should, in larger organisations, precede the annual budget cycle.

The best way to anchor a budget discussion is not by submitting a detailed strategic analysis to show why you should be targeting a doubling of sales volume. The best way is to talk very informally and very early on with the most senior people possible, before the strategic planning process even starts.

The coffee break anchor

Group CEO: 'Things look good this year...'

Business Unit Head (BUH): 'Next year could be even better. On current trends, 35 per cent growth is not impossible, if we have the resources to support it.'

CEO: '35 per cent? I thought we were on trend for nearer 10 per cent?'

BUH: '35 per cent assumes we invest in the new product stream that is coming on line...'

CEO: 'Sounds good, but cash flow will be a challenge...'

BUH: 'We'll look into it...'

Next year's budget discussion has just been anchored at 35 per cent growth, with the need to look hard at cash flow. Neither side has promised anything, yet. If this conversation had not happened, and instead the CEO had listened to the highly cautious CFO, the budget discussion could have been anchored around 10 per cent volume growth and a static budget.

Adjustments

Adjustments take the form of the question: 'What will be different next year from this year?' This is where there is intense negotiation on the detail. Adjustments look at incremental differences from this year: anchoring looks at step-change differences from this year. Typical incremental differences will include:

- productivity improvements
- inflation, salaries, etc.
- new initiatives and projects
- market and competitive trends
- pricing opportunities and pressures.

These discussions can be like trench warfare. Staff functions tend to have the advantage because they have the support and power of senior management on whose behalf they are acting. They are also working 100 per cent on budget discussions, while managers have to manage a business as well.

Consequently, many managers give up too easily. This is a mistake. It is better to have one tough month negotiating an easy budget than to have one tough year delivering a budget that was set too high.

> It is better to have one tough month negotiating an easy budget than to have one tough year delivering a budget that was set too high.

This debate is reversed from senior management's perspective. They know that there will be widespread game playing in the budget negotiations, with each budget holder having well-rehearsed arguments as to why the outlook is uniquely grim for the future and why delivering any sort of profit will be nearly impossible. There are two defences against this for senior managers:

1 **Staff warfare**: use the staff in planning and finance to run the process, challenge and check facts, and maintain a semblance of honesty in the debate.

2 **Be selectively unreasonable**: good managers are selectively unreasonable; reasonable managers listen to all the excuses as to why something is not possible. Any reasonable manager would have told Kennedy that his dream of putting a man on the moon within 10 years was not possible: the technology, skills, organisation and money simply did not exist. Reasonable managers would have been right in their assessment, and that is why they have been forgotten. Unreasonable managers demand outstanding performance and then support and enable it. Turning a deaf ear to excuses is a useful skill, even if it irritates the managers who are doing the special pleading.

Manage your budget

1 **Negotiate your budget**

   Do not wait for the budget to be dictated to you. Push early, push hard for a budget that you can deliver. Over-deliver against a soft budget; do not struggle with a challenging budget.

2 **Always deliver**

   Once you have accepted the budget, you are committed. Deliver.

3 **Front load performance**

   Surprises happen and they are rarely pleasant. Push hard in the first quarter/half to underspend on expenses and over-deliver on revenues.

4 **Spend discretionary budget early**

   Discretionary budget (conferences, research, test markets) will be confiscated from you in the final quarter as part of the inevitable year-end squeeze. It cannot be confiscated if you have already spent it.

5 **Watch the accruals**

   Always look forward, understand what commitments you have made. Make accurate projections to the end of the year, so you can take corrective action early, if necessary.

6 **Sandbag**

   Build a reserve for year end. Delay new hires for a couple of months, put their salaries in reserve.

7 **Squeeze**

   Get smart about spending. Challenge every line item: either squeeze it (cut suppliers' prices) or eliminate it completely.

8 **Protect your budget**

   Watch out for budget games: other departments transferring costs to you, increasing transfer prices, head office mandating services to you and charging. Deal with these territorial battles as you would deal with any external supplier: negotiate hard.

9 Act early

If you need to change course, do so early while you can still make budget. If you will miss, have a very good story and show what you will do to close the gap. Stay in control of the messaging and the plan.

10 Over-deliver (but not by too much)

If you are having a very good year, then sandbag in the final quarter: pull forward spending so that you do not underspend too much; delay revenues so you do not over-achieve too much. This keeps the baseline low for next year and allows you to have a very fast start to next year.

2.7 Managing budgets: the annual dance routine

Each year follows a predictable budget cycle. The year starts full of hope. Then there is a gradual squeeze. High-performing units suddenly have their goals raised even higher to make up for the shortfall in the weaker units. Weaker units start to get more help than they care for: being behind budget is an uncomfortable experience. This cycle shapes the way managers need to manage their budget.

- **Know your numbers in advance of the official data**. The purpose of this is to show that you are in control of the operation, and to take early corrective action if things are going off course. By the time you receive the report saying that your budget has crashed, it is too late. Accounting data looks backwards: you cannot drive the business forward by looking backwards. Most departments should be able to predict what will be happening three months in advance: sales will have a sales pipeline, HR will have a recruiting pipeline. Significant challenges caused by competitor activity, customers running into payment problems or major projects over-running should be visible to a manager who is in control. Use this sort of information to create your own early-warning radar system.

- **Prepare for a rainy day.** Two simple principles help here:

    1   The 48/52 rule is a simple discipline that calls for spending 48 per cent of your budget but achieving 52 per cent of your goals in the first six months of the financial year. This builds up some reserve for things going wrong later in the year. Even if things go wrong in the first half, the 48/52 rule means that your first half outcome still might be close to 50/50.

    2   Sandbag. You should have constructed your original budget so that you know where there is fat to be cut: maybe you know there is a supplier who can be squeezed further, or a project cost has been over-estimated, or a marketing campaign is a little too rich. The simplest way to sandbag is to delay a new hire for two–three months. You can pocket the budgeted salary payments as savings. Keep all your savings for a rainy day.

- **Manage communications well**. Follow three principles here:

    1   Avoid surprises. If there is bad budget news looming, prepare the way early and let top management know in advance about the challenge, and its cause and your proposed solution. Stay in control. If they call you asking you to explain a negative variance, you have a problem. You look like you were not in control, you are on the defensive and you are about to get the sort of staff and senior management help that no sane manager wants.

    2   Avoid boasting. It is human nature to brag when things are going well. It is senior management's nature to revise your budget upwards if they see things are going well. If things are going well, reset expectations low: show that the second half of the year will be much more challenging than the first half. Keep your original budget commitment for as long as possible.

    3   Do not whine; negotiate. If your budget revision is mandated from the top, use it to renegotiate your commitments. Do not offer something for nothing.

- **Prioritise your spending**. Phase spending carefully. There is a delicate balance to be achieved here. The reserving principle requires delaying expenditure. But the knowledge that budgets will become tighter later in the year requires bringing some spending forward. The spending to bring forward is a mixture of two elements:

  1 Essential investments for the business that may get cut later in the year – productivity investments that take time to pay back are vulnerable to a year-end squeeze.

  2 Discretionary spending that certainly will be cut in any squeeze, but that you need to build your team and its skills. Items such as conferences, training courses and laptop replacements are very easy to cut: if you believe they are important for any reason, spend the money before it is taken away.

All of these disciplines assume that you have accurate financial data. Perhaps the fastest way to lose credibility with an executive team is to produce unreliable data. If management cannot trust your data, they cannot trust you. It pays to have a good accountant on your team who can provide the information and the cover you need.

> If management cannot trust your data, they cannot trust you.

Budget utility and futility

Aged 18, I managed to find 10 weeks' work at the Inland Revenue (now HMRC). It was the employer of last resort and I was the employee of last resort. We were the perfect match.

The work itself was an education in futility. I had to alter, by hand, the tax codings of 10,000 taxpayers. This meant adding three numbers together to create a fourth number. The inefficiency was staggering:

- ten weeks' work took five weeks, at most
- the work could have been done in seconds by a computer
- the work was irrelevant anyway because the day after this annual ritual was completed, the Government would change the tax codings and the work would have to start all over again.

In week eight, my manager was in a great flap. He wanted me to do something, anything, to look busy. An inspector was coming and if he saw that I had already finished the ten-week task, he might conclude that ten weeks was too long. As a result, the manager's budget would be cut for the next year. So I looked busy, the manager kept his budget and I was given a pint of beer after work. Everyone was happy, except the long-suffering taxpayer: nothing new there, then.

I was starting to suspect that business and budgets were not all about efficiency and rationality. Politics and power seemed to be involved. But I assured myself that this was just the Inland Revenue. What else could you expect of a monopoly enforced by government? Surely other businesses and budgets would be far more rational and efficient with no hint of politics, wouldn't they?

2.8 Managing costs: minimising pain

Managing costs is at the heart of the management task. Inevitably, managers are squeezed. Input costs always go up: customers rarely volunteer price rises, staff rarely volunteer salary cuts, suppliers always want more and the tax inspector is always happy to steal another penny or two. On the other hand, there is the relentless logic of senior management and of the marketplace that demands betterfastercheaper: do not just cut costs, but do things better as well. People no longer accept a cost–quality trade-off. They want both.

This pressure builds up like clockwork towards the financial year end. The year starts full of hope. As it progresses, achieving targets becomes ever more challenging. One product or region hits a big problem, so the pain gets shared around the organisation: every other region and product has their goals raised to make up for the shortfall in the Japanese widgets market, the safety recall in Europe or the litigation in the United States.

By year end, management inevitably are looking at key ratios for the annual report. So expect the following demands:

- Cut costs, to meet budget. Cutting costs is easier, faster and more certain than raising revenues. And it feeds straight to the bottom line. It also creates problems for next year, but we will worry about next year, next year.

- Manage cash by squeezing suppliers (pay late) and customers (demand payment now).

- Get creative: capitalise expenditure, make some more exceptional provisions, delay major projects, recognise revenues as early as possible.

The astute manager knows that this squeeze is coming, and will prepare for it. That preparation comes in the form of a five-fold defensive strategy, outlined below. The purpose of cost cutting when it is part of the budget cycle is to do the minimum required to deliver the arbitrary demands of senior management and to avoid doing any substantive damage to the business itself. Short-term, budget-driven cost cuts are fundamentally different from the planned productivity improvements that all managers should seek anyway.

In recessions, cost cutting often is about survival, not productivity. The results can be ugly. The smartest firms use recessions to remove organisational tat and managerial low-flyers. Being smart is not a luxury all firms have in recessions.

Productivity is about real cost improvements; cost cuts driven by the annual budget cycle (as opposed to the panic of recession) involve considerable game playing by all levels of management.

The five levels of defence against the budget-driven cost-cutting demands are:

1 Play the game.

2 The soft squeeze.

3 The hard squeeze.

4 Make real change.

5 Pretend to make real change.

1 Play the game

Managers have three major tools to play with here. Each one of them is designed to avoid making any serious cost cuts that would harm the business.

1 **Sandbagging.** This is the gentle art of keeping as much in reserve and hidden from the prying eyes of management and staff for as long as possible. There is little point in squeezing suppliers mid-year: there will be nothing left to squeeze when top management insist on everyone delivering the 20 per cent improvement in payables and receivables by year end. This edict inevitably will punish the well-managed unit, while leaving the more politically astute unit with no real problems.

2 **KKK.** This is the Japanese alliteration for consultants, advertising and entertaining. In Japan, generally, they are considered easy and harmless things to cut. Each country and organisation will have its equivalent of KKK: it might be consultants, conferences and training. Naturally, if you have a conference to which you are really committed, make sure it is booked, paid for and non-refundable before the squeeze edict is issued.

3 **Timing.** Be prepared to delay costs or accelerate revenues. If you are having a really good year, work hard to accelerate costs and defer revenues: if you over-achieve this year, you will simply have a higher target next year. Better to start next year with a modest target but a very fast start in performance terms.

This game has to be played the right way. There are two common mistakes made when taking part:

1   Conceding to the new target too easily.

2   Whining about the new target. Telling management that it will be really hard to meet the target will make it feel good: you have just confirmed that you can meet the new target with hard work. Management likes managers to work hard and meet targets.

If you can, use the new target as an opportunity to negotiate. This is a way of making management understand that cutting costs has consequences, and it needs to deal with them. Cost cuts cannot be imagined out of thin air. There are two things you can try to ask for:

1   A delay in achieving a tough project that is close to the heart of management: this will test management resolve and give you more time to deliver. The excuse, of course, is that less budget means less support so more time is needed for completion.

2   A downwards revision in the goals for next year: underinvesting now has performance consequences later.

> If you do not ask the question, you do not get the answer.

Your success in renegotiating requires persistence, eloquence, political support and some luck. But, if you do not ask the question, you do not get the answer.

2 The soft squeeze

Once the game playing is over, you may have to deliver some real cost cuts. This soft squeeze goes through four levels of pain:

1   **Squeeze discretionary external staff and costs.** Look hard at temporary, contract and consulting staff. If necessary, show them the same level of loyalty that most of them have for you. Get rid of them. Start downgrading the class of travel. Corporate big shots will discover that turning right, not left, at the aircraft door does not lead to an instant heart attack.

2 **Squeeze internal discretionary staff.** Stop overtime. Start offering staff more work–life balance: flexi-time, sabbaticals and job sharing. As things get harder, extend the Christmas or summer shut-down periods.

3 **Put in a headcount freeze.** This normally requires making it very hard to hire replacement staff when someone leaves: you still need to find ways of putting extra staff into areas where they are most needed. So, if someone leaves, do not assume they can be replaced automatically: the effort of that head may be better used elsewhere.

4 **Put in a hiring freeze.** This now starts to cause pain. No leaving staff are replaced. Often the areas under the most pressure have the highest staff turnover, so a hiring freeze hurts most where you can least afford it. Reassigning staff is often difficult because the skills mix is not right. It is tough to sustain a hiring freeze, except for very short periods. Even at this stage, a manager will have kept as much of the team together as possible. Cutting the team is bad for morale and leaves the operation weakened.

An early sign of the soft squeeze is the coffee machine: it goes from being free to being paid for. The money saved is irrelevant to the corporate budget. The purpose of such acts is symbolic. They are meant to raise staff cost consciousness; more often, they simply lower staff morale.

3 The hard squeeze

This is where the pain really starts. The last ditch of defence is voluntary redundancy, which can be achieved in two ways:

1 **Raising the bar.** Raise the performance bar, and quietly counsel out the lower performers. This is an elegant solution that may increase the overall quality of the team and get rid of people who have not been contributing enough. In this respect, recessions are good. They enable some corporate house cleaning.

Recessions clear out poor businesses and poor managers alike. The problem is that this needs time: time to establish the performance track record (or lack of it) and time to ease people out. It works as a long-term management practice, but is difficult in response to a short-term cost-cutting drive.

2   **Asking for volunteers.** This tends to be a disaster. It is an admission that the ship is sinking, so the people who can swim will swim. The best people who can get jobs elsewhere will go. Anyone who cannot get a job elsewhere clings desperately to the sinking ship. This is precisely not the team you want to keep.

The final alternative is to make involuntary redundancies. This is clearly an organisation in some crisis. There is no kind way of firing people. As with executions, there are less cruel ways: doing it quickly is better than spinning out the agony for the victims. Let the unlucky people go with as much of their dignity intact as possible, and with as much hope for the future as possible. But the big trap is to focus too much on them. This sounds cruel, but you are going to have to live and work with the survivors, not the losers. It makes sense to invest as much time as possible in helping the survivors see that there is still hope, there is still a future and that they can be part of it.

4 Make real change

None of the cost-cutting efforts described above actually improve the underlying performance of the business. Knee-jerk cost cuts look impressive and help the CEO get a bigger bonus. But they do not help the business.

In practice, real change comes from two different angles:

1   **Steady operational improvement.** The *kaizen* approach of improving costs and quality a few per cent each year. Reducing costs by 4 per cent annually achieves more and is less painful than the once-in-five-years, macho 20 per cent cost cutting here.

2   **Strategic change.** This is about making structural change to
    the cost model: eliminating unprofitable and high-cost products,
    markets and channels; developing new technologies, products
    and markets; changing the competitive position. All of this looks
    very easy when written in a report but is very difficult to achieve.

One version of strategic change much loved by CEOs is financial
engineering: using the balance sheet to buy and sell businesses.
In good times buy, in recessions sell. When CEOs play the corporate equivalent of Monopoly, shareholders lose and bankers
win. Bankers get fees on the way up and on the way down – for
advising on purchases and sales and financing debt. Shareholders
lose by paying for over-priced assets in the boom and for selling
at fire-sale prices in the bust.

The problem with all the real changes is that all your competitors
are doing more or less the same with roughly as much skill and
talent as you. Each year you run harder and harder simply to stay
still compared to the competition. At least no one pretends that
management is easy.

5 Pretend to make real change

The need to make continual cost and productivity improvements
is real. Even the most successful organisations cannot stand still.
But the more successful an organisation is, the less managers will
feel the need to make painful decisions. Inevitably, therefore, they
will find ways of showing that they are making great improvements
while, in reality, they are achieving nothing. This sort of cost cutting
delivers red dollars: they look great but have no value compared to
green dollars. There are two basic ways of delivering red dollars:

1   **Squeezing the balloon.** Squeezing a balloon pushes air
    from one part of the balloon to another: it does not reduce
    the amount of air in it. Squeezing the corporate balloon
    transfers costs from one place to another to create a mirage of
    improvement. There are two ways of squeezing the balloon:

(a) Transfer costs to other departments: increase transfer prices, charge for previously free services (IT help desks, legal support, payroll administration, etc.).

(b) Transfer costs to another year: delay paying customers, delay major expenditures, capitalise costs (then pay depreciation on the new-found assets over the next five years).

2 **Score boarding.** This is a favourite of consultants and project managers who have to show results from their project. Again, there are two basic ways of score boarding:

(a) Count all the potential gains as real gains: the re-engineering project may have identified 20 per cent excess capacity across 50 people. But you cannot cut 20 per cent of each person. So the project leader agrees with the line manager that a 20 per cent (or 10 staff) cost reduction has been identified and then adds the 20 per cent to the long list of cost savings the project has achieved. With tedious regularity, senior management fails to follow up and check that the 20 per cent actually has been delivered by the line manager.

(b) Changing the baseline. If a department is looking for a 30 per cent increase in budget and then settles for a 15 per cent increase, be ready for the claim that it has cut its budget by 15 per cent. A 15 per cent increase has been converted into a 15 per cent cut. This ploy is greatly favoured by politicians when debating budgets.

Game playing like this is a sure sign of a fat and bloated organisation. Knowing how the games are played can help you spot and control them, or to play them, as conditions require.

The mysterious case of the missing $35 million

Head office calmly announced it was increasing its budget from an already outrageous $94 million to $134 million. That was $40 million of potential bonus money that it was stealing. When questioned on the number, it threw down a challenge: 'If anyone thinks they can reduce this very tough budget to less than $100 million, they are welcome to try.' Head office managers smirked, knowing that no one is dumb enough to make enemies of the whole of head office.

Well, more or less no one is that dumb. Unfortunately for them and for me, I was in the room. I volunteered for career suicide. The challenge was to find $35 million of apparent savings without creating mortal enemies of every powerful panjandrum in the business. Follow the red dollar dance:

- Use the wrong baseline: cutting a notional budget of $134 million is far easier than cutting real spending and real jobs from this year's budget of $94 million. I could cut $35 million and still leave head office with an increase in budget of over 5 per cent ($94 million to $99 million).

- Transfer costs: head office loved this. We started charging for everything, even the voicemail system. Out went the 0800 number, in came a regular toll number. The business was no better off in total, but head office was able to show a reduction in its net cost.

- Capitalise as many costs as possible: move head office to a site where we owned the freehold, and forget to charge rent. Huge apparent savings in expenditure. Extend the laptop replacement cycle from two years to four years.

The exercise officially saved $35 million. In practice, it achieved zero cost savings for the business. But it did save my career, so it was a very worthwhile exercise.

Setting and controlling budgets

1 **Be demanding**

Managers always want a soft budget and will find endless reasons why that should be so. You have to challenge and stretch them to improve.

2 **Make friends with the book keeper/accounts/finance**

These people can be your eyes and ears and can help you identify surprises before they hurt too much.

3 **Have clear controls**

Be clear about who is authorised to spend how much. Enforce controls rigorously. But do not micro manage: trust your managers with some budget discretion. You do not have to authorise each photocopy.

4 **Stick to the process**

You will hear many excuses for why expenses are late, the month end close has been missed and the accounts are out of date. If your data is bad and out of date, you cannot manage well. Enforce the process and the standards.

5 **Hold managers to account: the budget is the budget is the budget**

Hold regular (monthly) reviews where managers can explain variances and agree any corrective action. You will hear endless reasons why the budget should change. But once your team has committed to a budget, that is their contract with you. Hold them to their contract.

6 **Steal any cost savings**

Inevitably, some departments will miss budget. So you have to rebalance across departments: that means you have to keep any cost savings.

7 **Focus on accruals, not cash**

Spending is not just cash: it is also about commitments to future spending. Control commitments as you control cash. Make projections based on commitments.

8 Watch the big items, not the small

It is easier to control the small items like the cost of photocopying. The big items like payroll are harder to control, but that is why you are a manager: to do the hard work.

9 Be flexible about the means

As much as you are rigid about the goals, be flexible about how you get there. Trust your team to be creative. Help them achieve the goal.

10 Watch for game playing

You played all the games as a manager, so you know the tricks: sandbagging, delaying new hires, hiding costs and revenues over the year end. You may decide to play along or oppose them, but at least make an informed choice.

2.9 Surviving spreadsheets: assumptions, not maths

In the days before spreadsheets, there was a naive assumption that good maths equalled good thinking and dodgy maths equalled dodgy thinking.

In the spreadsheet era, we do not have to worry about dodgy maths so much, unless someone is using elaborate equations. Understanding spreadsheets is about good thinking, not good maths. It pays to understand how the spreadsheet was created. The person producing the spreadsheet deploys two basic tactics:

1 **Start at the bottom right-hand corner.** You know the answer must be x% or £y million. So keep on adjusting the spreadsheet inputs until **x** or **y** is achieved. Then add a safety margin and make sure the number does not look suspiciously round.

2   **Overwhelm the opposition (senior managers and staffers) with data**. About 200 lines and 40 columns of data over 6 interrelated pages should scare off most people, especially when all they really want to see is whether the number in the bottom right-hand corner of the spreadsheet looks good: **x** or **y** with a bit of safety margin built in.

The rules for the spreadsheet survival game are very simple, and are completely different if you are writing the spreadsheet or are reading it.

The rules for the spreadsheet writer are as follows:

● Start with the desired answer in the bottom right-hand corner.

● Work out whatever scenarios and assumptions justify getting to the answer.

● Make minor but easily checked assumptions very conservative, so that you appear not to be reckless and have evidence to show you are careful.

● Cover your tracks: leave some safety margin and avoid round numbers.

● Get key people to validate the key assumptions in your model, so that senior management cannot pick it apart. Validation is the most painful, but useful, part of the exercise: it is employed in the process of checking assumptions with sales, marketing, HR, finance and other relevant experts to gain insight, test thinking and build credibility for later.

For the spreadsheet reader, the rules are largely reversed:

● Ignore the answer, unless it is not what you want to see. Assume it has been fudged.

● Before you look at the spreadsheet, think of the five major assumptions that will drive the outcome, and note what reasonable might look like for each one.

● Before you look at the spreadsheet, ask the spreadsheet writer what assumptions he or she has made for the five major drivers you have identified. You may well have a lively discussion at this point.

● Ask 'What if…' questions: What if each of the major assumptions lands up being different from what you are expecting? Where are the risks? How can you mitigate those risks? Create some scenarios based on changing assumptions. This is a basic sensitivity analysis. Never rely on a single point solution: look at multiple scenarios.

● Only now is it worth actually looking at the spreadsheet.

2.10 Knowing numbers: playing the numbers game

Numbers make many people feel nervous. With a degree in history, numbers certainly made me feel nervous. I was not even much good at historical dates. The critical breakthrough came in discovering that management numbers are not about maths: they are about thinking and persuasion. Even historians can manage that, on a good day. In contrast, not all mathematicians feel confident about business thinking and persuasion. The numbers game is an equal-opportunity challenge for all disciplines: it is equally tough for everyone.

> Management numbers are not about maths: they are about thinking and persuasion.

There are four major variations of the numbers game:

1 The assumptions game.

2 The averages game.

3 The baseline game.

4 The validation game.

1 The assumptions game

This is how to look smart whenever presented with a complex spreadsheet or proposal. Do not worry about the maths.

Look at the largest figures and then test the assumptions behind them. This has been covered fully in spreadsheet survival above. Typical assumptions to test involve:

- the market: size, growth, share
- customers: number, cost to acquire, cost to serve, attrition
- operations: cost per job, overhead per person, property, systems
- people: number required, cost per person, cost to hire, attrition.

The way to succeed at this game is to create your own checklist of assumptions before you even see the spreadsheet or proposal. Do not get caught up in the Byzantine internal logic of the proposal in front of you. If you make sure your own thinking and assumptions are clear, it becomes easy to test other people's thinking and assumptions.

2 The averages game

Averages are profoundly misleading. The average human is 51 per cent female and has fewer than two legs (some people have lost legs). Useless. Average customer satisfaction is 3.2 on a 5-point scale. Utterly useless. Of far more use to a manager are the extremes and the segments, for example:

- If average customer satisfaction is 3.2, how many are really happy and how many really unhappy with us? Why? How many of the unhappy ones leave us? How can we make the happy ones even more happy? Does average satisfaction cover up delight with one thing we do (in-store service) and disgust with another (telephone support)?
- The average (possibly median or mean, but we will let that distinction pass) household income is $58,000 in the United States. So what? Does this mean that there is no market for private jets or upmarket hotels and holidays?

- The average temperature of someone with their head in the oven and their feet in the freezer is probably quite acceptable. Do not try this experiment at home (or elsewhere).

When faced with an average, always look for the extreme scores behind the average, and the major segments around the average: that is where the real insight will come from.

Sneezing at averages

The car was full of a new toilet soap that we were going to launch nationally. It had an overpowering fragrance, which made everyone in the car sneeze. After four hours of driving and sneezing, we hated it as much as the consumers in our market research. And we were its managers. We wondered how a toilet soap that scored so low in research could go national. The answer was that, in the test market, it had done very well. This made the riddle even more confusing.

The market research was based on all consumers, most of whom hated it, even if they were not sneezing at it. But about 15 per cent of the population thought it was brilliant, the best toilet soap they had ever tried. Given that no toilet soap had more than 10 per cent of the market, this was extremely good news. Following the market research, we put the soap into test market and the 15 per cent of diehards duly bought the soap in vast quantity and at great expense.

The average reaction to our product was irrelevant. We had a profitable hit on our hands, based on one segment of the market. Now all we had to do was to sneeze our way to the national sales conference...

3 The baseline game

Beating baselines is a classic intellectual and political challenge for managers. Setting a baseline ought to be a rational and objective exercise. It is not. It is a political exercise that fundamentally affects perceptions of performance. Naive managers ignore this and accept given baselines: experienced managers understand that the right performance baseline makes beating the baseline much easier than accepting a challenging baseline.

The two key variations of this game are:

1   The declining baseline.

2   The false baseline.

1 The declining baseline

> A baseline is, perhaps, the most deceptive and dangerous assumption in business.

A baseline is, perhaps, the most deceptive and dangerous assumption in business. It is deceptive because it seems so natural and reasonable, and it is dangerous because it is often wrong. Spot what is wrong in these two cases.

- **Case one**. Our current budget is £15 million a year. We have worked very hard and we have identified cost savings of 15 per cent. Even allowing for 5 per cent inflation, that means we can deliver about 10 per cent cost savings. That means £1.5 million for the bottom line. Can I have my bonus please?

- **Case two**. Our market share is 10 per cent. We have decided to reinvest the cost savings from case one into a major price reduction. We know from market research and from a small test market we did that a 10 per cent price reduction in this price-sensitive market will have a dramatic effect and we will increase our market share to 15 per cent. This is such a scale-sensitive business that growth will be highly profitable.

The fallacy in both cases is to assume that the baseline is stable over time. The starting point of the current budget or market position is never stable over time. In business, all such baselines are on a continual downwards trend. Competitors wreck our plans by improving their efficiency and cutting costs as well. Competitors will match our efforts in both case one and case two:

we will make the cost savings as promised, but there will be no increase in profit or market share as long as the competition does as well as we do. We are running hard to stay still.

Even without the effect of competition, organisations still face a declining baseline. Every organisation slowly slides towards chaos: experienced staff leave and new staff come in who need training; suppliers mess up; customer demands change; technology makes our current ways of working redundant; machines and systems break down; events happen. Against this background, huge effort is required simply to keep things in a steady state. The consequences of this are significant:

- Cost-savings programmes rarely result in profit improvements: all the savings get competed away by equally vigorous competitors. Only customers gain from your efforts.

- Sales and marketing programmes struggle to build market share, given the effects of competition.

- Managers have to run hard to stay still: doing as well as last year takes enormous effort to cope with the adverse effects of competition and the internal forces of entropy, which work against success.

2 The false baseline

The false baseline is used by managers at all levels, and in particular by CEOs. It is the natural, political response to the problem of the declining baseline. The purpose of the false baseline is to set the starting point so low that anything you do has to be an improvement on where you are today.

When you inherit a job, you may well find that the person who preceded you has left a picture of a great job brilliantly done, which is why they were promoted. They will have shown that they had put in place all the plans required to transform the business. If you allow that propaganda to flourish, you are finished. If you succeed, it will be because of the plans that the previous incumbent put in place. If you do less than brilliantly, it will be because you messed up. You do not want to inherit a baseline set impossibly high.

The alternative is to show, as fast as possible, that the job or department you inherited is on the brink of collapse. Everything is a disaster, which only a superhero can possibly turn around, but luckily you have arrived in the nick of time. If things now proceed modestly well, you will have done a great job in averting disaster.

The same modest performance can be seen as a disaster or as a triumph, depending on how the baseline was set.

4 The validation game

The validation game is about people and politics as much as it is about numbers. Venture capitalists, bankers and senior managers do not simply look at the numbers being presented to them. They look at the people behind the numbers. A solid proposal from a team with high credibility is more convincing than an exciting proposal from a weak team.

Effective managers understand this and will use it to their advantage. Validation is required from two sources. First, get the sheriff and his deputies on board. You can find them in marketing, HR, IT, finance and accounting. They will all want their say. Let them have it, in private. Let them nitpick in private. As soon as anyone takes a public position, they find it very hard to change. Their position is public if they state it in a meeting where more than two people are present. The important thing is to get them on your side, in private. Once you have the sheriff on board, approach the mayor. The mayor is the local power broker. Whereas the sheriff and deputies are interested in the detail of their individual areas, the mayor is interested in the bigger picture: how your numbers fit with all the other priorities and numbers in town.

Once you have lined up the sheriff, deputies and mayor to support you, you can really go to town and have fun. The other cowboys will not even get a look-in.

Chapter 3

Emotional management skills:

dealing with people

EQ is not about being nice for the sake of being nice. Organisations are not created to deliver niceness. Organisations are created to deliver results, which in the case of private-sector companies normally come in the form of profits. EQ is not an end in itself. It is a means to an end.

EQ is about knowing how to get other people to do things: this places it at the heart of management. EQ is not the same as command and control. It is about being able to use influence to get other people to do things willingly, regardless of whether or not you have formal control over them. To make things happen in most flat, matrix organisations it is not possible to tell people to do things: you have no control over them. You have to find ways of working with them that gain their active support and commitment. If you can do this, you will wield power and have effectiveness, which goes far beyond your official job title.

EQ is not an innate characteristic that either you have or do not have. There are many managers who think they are very good with people. They may even be right. But being liked is not the same thing as being respected and valued in a business context. Effective managers need to be respected and trusted: they do not need to be liked. This is not a new insight. Machiavelli (1469–1527) advises his Prince that 'it is better to be feared than loved, if you cannot be both'. He then recommends a few exemplary

> Effective managers need to be respected and trusted: they do not need to be liked.

executions to maintain order. While such drastic action is not always necessary, the fate of many likeable people is salutary: you often find them languishing in organisational backwaters where their ineffectiveness does not matter.

Learning EQ starts with a Copernican revolution. Copernicus discovered that Planet Earth is not the centre of the universe. EQ starts with the discovery that we are not at the centre of the universe. Effective EQ requires that we can see the world through the eyes of other people. We do not have to like what we see or agree with it. But we must understand others' perspectives. Only when we understand their view of the world can we hope to change it.

EQ is best learned as a series of discrete skills, which have immediate relevance to essential management tasks. The skills-based approach to EQ is simple and practical. In the following sections, this chapter will focus on ten EQ-based skills that are at the heart of management.

Motivating people: creating willing followers

Persuading people: how to sell anything

Coaching: no more training

Delegating: doing better by doing less

Handling conflict: from FEAR to EAR

Giving informal feedback: making the negative positive

Using time effectively: activity versus achievement

Minding your mind: the management mindset

Find your performance zone: learn to thrive

Learning the right behaviours: what your team really wants

The alert reader may wonder if persuading and motivating people are different: they are. Persuading people often is an event. It is about gaining other people's support for an idea or course of action. It is, effectively, a transaction between two people where one person persuades or influences the other person. Motivating people is not about a single transaction: it is about creating a longer-term relationship in which the properly motivated person will do things without having to be told or asked to do them. Well motivated, they will go above and beyond expectations and do more than is strictly necessary.

The truly critical reader will have noticed the omission of topics such as change management and political awareness. These are covered in detail under PQ, which focuses on how the manager and the organisation interact: EQ focuses more on how the manager and other individuals interact.

Without further ado, let us look at each of these EQ-heavy skills.

3.1 Motivating people: creating willing followers

The basic theories

After a few hundred thousand years of human existence, we may, finally, be working out what motivates people. To find the answer, we will look first at two theories that continue to dominate management thinking. Then we will look at management practice.

For the first theory, imagine any work group that you particularly dislike inside or beyond your organisation. Then imagine a group with which you particularly enjoy working. Which of the following two descriptions best fits each group you have chosen?

Description X

They are, essentially, lazy and work-shy. They work mainly for the money, which they will maximise. They will minimise the amount of effort, doing only what is consistent with avoiding disciplinary action or loss of earnings. They dislike risk, ambiguity and responsibility. They like leaving all the tough decisions to other people: then they get to complain about

▶

the stupid decisions that have been made on their behalf. The best way to control these people is through close monitoring, clear rewards and sanctions, and unambiguous direction.

Description Y

With proper management, these people can be committed: they will work hard and use some degree of creativity to overcome problems without seeking direction; they will seek responsibility rather than avoid it and clearly get more out of work than just a monthly salary. These people can be trusted with delegated tasks, do not need close supervision and will learn and grow in their jobs.

The chances are that you can identify people who belong to both groups. Each group needs to be managed in a different way. In theory, Type X individuals characterised the nineteenth century sweatshop full of unskilled labour, and Type Y individuals characterise the twenty-first century highly skilled and highly motivated workforce in advanced economies. In practice, both sorts can be found in all kinds of environments. There is also a large element of self-fulfilment here. If you treat people as if they cannot be trusted and need to be controlled, they will start responding to Type X management with Type X behaviour: they will do the minimum to comply with you, but they will demonstrate little commitment. Equally, start managing in Type Y style, and people are likely to respond positively.

These two types of individual were described by McGregor in *The Human Side of Enterprise* (1960). Over 50 years later, the idea of Type X managers (close control, tough managers) and Type Y managers (delegating, trusting types) still exists. The big insights from Type X and Type Y have the virtue of simplicity:

- Different people need to be managed in different ways.
- Most managers are biased towards either Type X or Type Y.

Therefore, managers either need to find the right context where their style works, or they need to be able to adapt their style to different situations. Think of most managers you have worked with: very few are able to switch between Type X and Type Y. Style conflicts are at the heart of most dysfunctional team management problems.

1 The sophisticated theories

If you want to be sophisticated, you need something a bit more fancy than a straight choice between two alternatives, which is as simple as tossing a coin and calling 'X' or 'Y'. So move aside McGregor and make way for Maslow. Maslow developed the hierarchy of needs in a series of articles and books from 1943 (*A Theory of Human Motivation*) to 1997 (*Motivation and Personality*). It pays to know about Maslow because:

- his name and his thinking pervade much management thought
- some of his thinking is genuinely useful.

Maslow's fundamental insight is that we are all needs junkies. There is always something more that we want. Once we have satisfied one level of need, we find there is something more that we want. As children, we want a push bike, then we want a motorbike, then a car; to keep up with colleagues, we graduate to a sports car, then a private jet to keep up with other CEOs and, finally, we need our own personal jumbo jet. We laugh at anyone left on their push bike. Maslow came at this from a psychological background. Economists notice the same effect and call it hedonic adaptation: we adjust up to a higher standard of living more easily than we adjust down. If you were happy 20 years ago, think if you would still be happy without your iPad, smart phone, computer, internet

> If you were happy 20 years ago, think if you would still be happy without your iPad, smart phone, computer, internet connection and cheap flights.

connection and cheap flights. Quite how anyone survived 20 years ago is a mystery.

At the bottom of Maslow's pyramid (see the figure below) are deficiency needs: if we do not have food, water and air (physiological needs), we are likely to be unhappy. Safety is also a deficit need: we are unhappy without shelter and protection. At the top of the pyramid we have growth needs. We want to find meaning and leave a legacy. Much of this echoes the work of other psychologists, and is not greatly controversial. Having said that, Maslow's categories are dangerously close to psychobabble and are largely useless in a management context. Asking the CEO if he is at the love stage is open to misinterpretation. Knowing what stage people are at and knowing what to do about it are not obvious.

Managers need something easier and more practical. So here (in the figure opposite) is a revisionist, unauthorised alternative to Maslow's hierarchy of needs: the management hierarchy of needs.

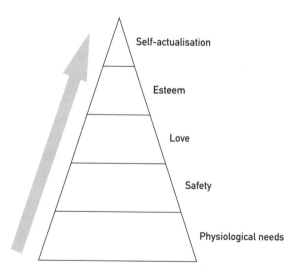

Maslow's hierarchy of needs
Source: Maslow, A.H. (1943) 'A theory of human motivation', *Psychological Review* 50(4), 370–96. This content is in the public domain.

The management hierarchy of needs

This starts to be easier to work with. In boom times, staff may be lobbying for greater recognition and reward. They may have lofty thoughts of the legacy they will deliver. In recession, people become very interested in job security and will even sacrifice some pay and conditions just to survive. Maslow makes sense over the business cycle. In normal times, pay and conditions are unlikely to make people happy, but getting them wrong can make people unhappy.

Bonus time!

Working with an investment bank at bonus time was a revelation. One senior trader was given a $300,000 bonus, which would be enough for most people. He quickly resigned in disgust (pausing only to deposit the cheque into his account). A close colleague had received $500,000. The problem was that the money was recognising him as less valuable than his colleague. For an executive who was clearly at the recognition and reward stage of his career, this was a terrible blow to his fragile, supersized ego.

At a basic level, a manager can use this framework to see if the basic conditions are in place for having a motivated team:

- Do people have a sense of security, or is there constant fear, uncertainty and doubt?
- Are the pay and conditions fair and appropriate?
- Do team members feel part of a team and a community, or is it survival of the fittest?
- Are team members recognised for their contributions, or is all the limelight hogged by one or two?
- Are there worthwhile goals for the team as a whole, and do those goals support the personal aspirations of each individual?

If you can answer these questions positively, you have gone a long way to creating the conditions for a motivated team. But you have not gone all the way: motivation is not about systems on bits of paper. Motivation is an engagement sport: you have to deal with people, not paper, to motivate humans. There will be some managers who turn this hierarchy on its head and rule by fear and constant threats. People may have to work *for* such bosses to pay the mortgage. Few people choose to work *with* such bosses.

2 Motivation practice: the magic rule

Maslow helps us understand only how to create the preconditions for a motivated team. He does not tell us how to deal with people on a day-to-day and minute-to-minute basis.

In practice, motivation is happening positively or negatively all the time. Small actions and a few words can raise or lower the motivation thermostat for each individual fast. This means managers have to react quickly and well to constantly changing situations: humans are not as predictable as computers.

To find out what made a good manager, we assessed all the managers in our organisation and then asked their teams to assess the managers as well. There was a mountain of data, which was largely indigestible and very confusing. But the more we looked, the more we found that there was one question that accurately predicted how well each manager would be rated by his or her team for intelligence, decision-making ability, charisma, organisational skills, team leadership and all the other qualities we looked for. The question was:

'My boss cares about me and my career' (agree/disagree).

This was so simple and so obvious. People want to be cared for, valued and respected as individuals. Do this, and they will repay your efforts many times over. So, the emerging golden rule for motivation is:

Show you care about the future of each individual on your team.

Caring is not about being sugar-sweet nice all the time and one-minute managing people with empty compliments. It takes commitment and hard work on both sides. It involves the following qualities, which will be covered in more detail in later sections:

- **Listening**: ask open questions and understand the answers before trying to judge people.
- **Coaching**: help people deal with challenges themselves; do not do it for them.
- **Honesty**: deal with uncomfortable truths rather than hide them.
- **Delivery**: always deliver on your half of the psychological contract.
- **Style**: respect the different styles and skills of each team member – work with them rather than force them to fit your style.
- **Vision and direction**: make your department's vision relevant to each individual's personal needs, vision and direction.

If this sounds like hard work, it is. But it is hard work with a purpose: to encourage each team member to contribute to the greatest of his or her ability. And if it all sounds a little complicated, it can be made simple. Even trying to show you care has an immediate impact.

How to manage professionals

1 **Stretch them**

   Professionals are natural over-achievers. Let them over-achieve, learn and grow. An idle professional is a dangerous professional.

2 **Set a direction**

   Professionals do not respect weak managers: set a direction, be clear about how you will get there and stick to it.

3 **Shield your team**

   Focus your team on where they can make a difference. Shield them from the politics, routine rubbish and noise of corporate life. They may even be grateful to you if you do this well.

4 **Support your team**

   Set the team up for success: make sure they have the right resources, right support and right goal.

5 **Show you care**

   Invest time in each team member: understand their needs and expectations. Help them on their career journey.

6 **No surprises**

   Do not surprise your team at appraisal time: all trust will be lost. Have difficult performance conversations early so they can change course.

7 **Recognise them**

   Professionals have pride. Feed their egos: praise good work in public. Never, never demean them in public. Have the hard conversations in private.

8 Delegate

If in doubt, delegate everything. Do not let them delegate problems back up to you. Coach them to solve the problem themselves: they will learn and be more valuable team members as a result.

9 Set expectations

Some professionals want it all and want it now. Some want more and sooner. Any half comment about bonus and promotion will be taken as a 100 per cent firm promise. Be clear and consistent in your messaging.

10 Manage less

Trust your team. Manage by walking away. Micro managing shows lack of trust and builds resentment among professionals. Trust your team and they will rise to the challenge.

3.2 Persuading people: how to sell anything

Managers need to influence people in the flat world of the matrix organisation: managers lack the power to tell people what to do, so they persuade people to do things. Managers are, effectively, sales people: they sell ideas, priorities, changes and solutions to other departments, even if they are not selling products and services to customers.

> Managers are, effectively, sales people.

1 The principles of persuading people

Fear, greed, idleness and risk may not be the most uplifting guides to human behaviour but, in management terms, they work with unerring accuracy. These are the four dimensions you need to use to influence someone (see the figure overleaf). People want to escape fear, strive for something (greed and hope) but face the two barriers of risk and idleness. A good influencer knows how to play on all four of these dimensions.

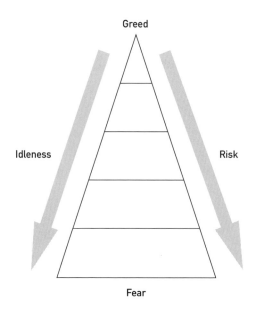

Maslow reduced

Greed

Greed corresponds to Maslow's growth needs: everyone wants something and, when they get it, they want something more. To start with, they may want money. But greed is not just about money. People want other things. People like to be recognised. It may be something as simple as praise in public for a job well done. Or it can be the ambitious business person seeking political recognition and public honour through good works and political donations. Effective managers need to find out what the other person wants.

In daily management practice, greed can be translated into the everyday hopes of colleagues. They have goals and deadlines to meet. They want to look good and to succeed. It does not matter how brilliant your idea may be; if it does not help your colleagues with their agendas you can expect a lukewarm response. Your idea may look great to you: it looks like more work for them.

Fear

Fear is the other side of the coin to greed. It can be a very compelling way of gaining compliance with your idea. In many cases, the proposal is simple: 'If you do not do this the consequences will be…' At the first mention of regulatory, legal, health and safety concerns, many managers give up: it is not worth taking the risk of letting these things go wrong, even if the risk is very small and the cost is very large. Playing to fear is also used by IT consultants: if you do not implement our very expensive project, then all your mission critical programmes are at risk. Many senior executives lack the technical expertise or will to argue against such fear-based selling.

Fear is also relative. Cost-cutting programmes normally increase fear, not reduce it. That is one reason they are resisted overtly or covertly. To build support for cost-cutting programmes, senior executives play up the even greater fear of what happens if we do not cut costs now. If we do not cut costs now, we might all lose our jobs as the company goes bankrupt: better to lose a few people now than to lose everyone later.

Idleness

There are many things we would like to do. But life is busy. We might want to learn Spanish, get fit, become a painter and get involved in the community. But these things take effort and, in the meantime, we have the bills to pay, the dog to feed and the car has broken down again. At work, you have your great idea. But everyone else has other problems to attend to: budgets, meetings, deadlines and crises. Your idea is one more item on an already overcrowded list. Colleagues may like your idea, but not enough to stop working on their priorities to help you achieve yours.

You have to make it easy for people to accept your idea. Show how your idea will make it easier for them to achieve their goals by showing the opposite scenario: opposing your idea will take

> **You have to make it easy for people to accept your idea.**

up huge amounts of their time and will result in lost opportunities. Make it difficult for them to say no.

Risk

Risk is the iceberg that sinks many ideas. It is often unseen and unspoken. Most people are naturally risk averse. Any new idea inevitably carries all sorts of risks with it: it may not work; it may divert resources from other things; it may have unintended consequences; it may lead to a change in the power structure. At any meeting, listen to what happens when any new idea is raised (unless the idea comes from the boss). Immediately, people will start asking helpful questions along the lines of 'Have you thought of this or that...?' These helpful ideas have the effect of:

- showing that the questioner is listening and smart because he or she can identify problems fast
- killing the idea, because everyone sees how risky it is
- killing off innovation, because now everyone realises that to have an idea is to invite being shot down in public by intellectual questioning.

This is an unproductive outcome that could be avoided if people focused on the benefits and opportunities of an idea, before focusing on all the risks and problems, unhelpfully disguised as asking helpful questions.

Risk comes in three main flavours:

1 **Rational risk**: how will this affect the business? People are encouraged to discuss this openly, because business people are meant to be rational.

2 **Political risk**: how will this idea affect my department? Will it lose or gain resources, priorities and influence as a result of this idea?

3 **Emotional risk**: how will this idea affect me? Will I have to work harder, be marginalised, and have to work with a new

boss or develop new skills? People will never raise these risks in public. Instead, they will raise ever more persuasive rational and business objections, which are a cover for their personal and emotional objections.

It pays to know what sort of risk you are dealing with. Many arguments become increasingly bitter over apparently logical issues. When this happens, both sides start digging ever deeper holes, using logic to defend political and emotional positions. The best solution is to stop digging. Stop the discussion and find some time in private when the real issues can be raised and dealt with.

As with idleness, it pays to reverse the risk equation. Like fear, risk is relative. Show, if possible, that the risks of doing nothing significantly outweigh the risks of doing what you propose. Risk avoidance is a powerful way of gaining compliance. Insurance is sold entirely on the idea of risk avoidance. Government cannot persuade us to pay taxes or wear seat belts, but it makes the risks of not doing so high enough so that most people comply.

> Like fear, risk is relative.

Influencing people

1 **Build rapport**

Find common ground, common interests, common experience.

2 **Align your agendas**

Find out how they see the world, what they need, want and fear. Work your agenda to fit with theirs: do not start with your agenda and mindlessly inflict it on them.

3 **Listen**

The more you listen, the more you find out about them and the more they relax. Smart questions work better than smart ideas.

4 **Flatter**

There is no point at which flattery becomes counterproductive: no one thinks they are over-promoted, over-recognised and over-paid. If you recognise their innate genius, diligence and humanity, they will be in awe of your very fine judgement and will reciprocate.

5 **Build commitment incrementally**

Do not ask for everything all at once: do not scare them. Ask for small commitments and limited involvement. Let the commitments build.

6 **Build your trust and credibility**

Always deliver on your commitments.

7 **Manage risk**

People are risk averse. Remove perceived risk and personal risk; show that you can be trusted to deliver on commitments.

8 **Put scarcity to work**

Find something they want that you can give. And then make them work for it: they will value it more than if you give it away.

9 **Something for something: reciprocity works**

Do not give something for nothing: it sets the wrong expectations.

10 **Act the part: the partnership principle**

Act as their partner and equal, not as a supplicant. You want an adult to adult conversation, not a parent to child conversation.

2 The process of persuading people

This is a process that I have used to sell nappies in Birmingham, to sell the idea of starting a new bank, and to get countless recommendations accepted in different organisations and countries. The process combines a logical and emotional flow designed to make it easy for the other person to agree, and difficult for them to disagree. The flow is not original: it is based on the sales disciplines that Procter & Gamble instils in its sales force.

The process has an acronym: PASSION, which stands for:

Preparation

Alignment

Situation

Size the prize

Idea

Overcome objections

Next steps

Think of the PASSION principle as a series of traffic lights: do not proceed to the next part of the conversation until the lights have turned green at each step, otherwise you are likely to crash. It is a simple framework that allows you to work in the style you like: it is not a script you have to follow like a call centre operator.

Preparation

Preparation is about asking some basic questions:

● What are the benefits of my idea to the other person?

● What are the risks from their perspective?

● How can I make it easy for them to agree?

● What is their style of working, and how can I get along with them best?

● What is the best time to approach them?

● Have I got all the material I need to support my discussion with them?

● Do I know the logistics of the meeting: where, when and how to get there?

These are very obvious questions. They are very rarely asked, and you can look surprisingly smart by asking them when a team member comes and seeks your advice on how to plan an influencing meeting. Although the questions may be obvious, the answers often are not: many of them are about understanding the other person's hopes, fears, needs and wishes. If you do not understand this, you do not understand what you are selling.

Alignment

A truism among sales people is that you have to sell yourself before you can sell your idea. We buy only from people we trust. You also need to make sure that the other person is in the right frame of mind to listen: if they are frantically trying to put out fires in their area, they may not want to listen to your great idea.

The process of alignment can take a few seconds if you already know each other well. In this case, alignment is complete when you know:

● you are meeting at a convenient time

● you have anchored the meeting around the core topic

● you have built some trust and rapport with the other person.

This social start needs only a few questions and statements, such as:

● 'Thank you for meeting me. Is this still a convenient time?'

● 'You look as busy as ever' (inviting them to download their problems for a moment to an empathetic ear: if they are too busy, you will find out now).

● 'As promised, I have come to ask your advice about...'
    You have now anchored the conversation, and you have not put yourself into selling mode: you are asking for advice and help.

If you are meeting someone for the first time, alignment will take longer. You will need to build some rapport and trust. You can do this by finding a common interest, common acquaintances or common professional background. The purpose of such social chat is to build a basic level of trust by finding common experiences, values and outlooks.

Situation: agree the problem or opportunity

This is where most persuading goes wrong or right. You cannot get to the right solution if you do not know what the question is.

> You cannot get to the right solution if you do not know what the question is.

As with exams, it pays to know what the right question is. The classic mistake is to think that your problem or opportunity is the problem or opportunity that the other person wants to deal with. In reality, they have many other things to worry about. Buying the dog food may be more important to them than dealing with your issue.

Good influencing does not start with your idea. It starts with what the other person wants. You can preach as much as you want about your brilliant and urgent idea, but you may as well preach to the wall if you do not understand where the other person is coming from. So, if you want to influence well, start by listening and not by preaching.

Knowing what to sell: products versus solutions

History is littered with brilliant ideas that failed. Clive Sinclair, a British boffin, developed a vehicle called the C5. It was all-electric and would revolutionise urban transport. It might have done, if anyone had been able to stop laughing at the bug-like vehicle that was so low to the ground that it needed a flag at its rear end to alert other road users to its presence. And it could carry only one person, and it was open to the elements, and it had a limited range. It was technically brilliant but completely failed to solve a customer need. It disappeared faster than its backers' funding into a black hole.

The purpose of agreeing the problem is to force attention and gain legitimacy for the issue, which can be:

- **rational**: there is a big challenge for the whole organisation and we have the numbers to show it
- **emotional**: I can help you with your agenda and challenges
- **political**: we have to sort this out for our common boss.

To make the problem compelling, you have to show that it is important, urgent and that the other person has a role to play in sorting it out.

Do not even start to suggest a solution until there is hard agreement about the nature of the challenge. Invite them to talk about it: hear and understand their perspective. As you listen, you can work out how to pitch your idea so that it hits all the right buttons and avoids the red flags, which might stop the idea from their perspective.

You need to identify not just the problem, but who owns the problem. If you are helping the other person with one of their challenges, you are more likely to find an open door and an available diary than if you are solving your own problem.

Size the prize: outline the benefits of resolving the problem

In business, the most compelling business case is financial. It is very hard to argue against a credible and compelling business case: '£1,000 invested now will save £2,000 tomorrow.' The critical issue is whether anyone believes the claim. The claim must be credible. This can be achieved through a combination of rigorous analysis and, more importantly, validation by trusted third parties: finance validates the financial numbers, marketing validates the customer and market assumptions, and operations and IT validate their parts of the equation.

Not all benefits are financial. Non-financial business cases can be both quantifiable ('we will recruit more top graduates next year') and qualitative ('this is important for morale').

At this point, there still should be no mention of your idea or solution. Once the other person has agreed to both the problem and the benefits of solving the solution, then the only discussion is 'How do we best get there?' Then they are ready to hear your idea: even if they do not like it, they are now in a position where they are not just trying to evaluate your idea, but they are helping you find a path from the problem to the solution.

Idea

Provide a simple explanation of your idea. Keep it short. Show that you do not need them to do everything: you need a limited amount of support in one critical area to progress. Then quickly move on to the next stage.

If you have listened well in steps one to four, you will be able to frame your idea in the language of the other person, and you will be able to show how it helps them. Suggest your idea only when you are confident that you understand the other person and that they are ready to agree with you.

Overcome objections

If you have done your preparation well, and you listened to them when you were discussing the original problem, this should be easy: you should know exactly what their concerns are. Do not hide from these objections: use them as a chance to shine. If you now say: 'I think there are three real concerns with this approach...' and these concerns reflect the major concerns of the other person, suddenly you will have them on your side. They are no longer going to have to challenge you with their objections: you are inviting them to work with you on solving the concerns. The nature of the discussion has changed completely. You have changed your role from being a pesky salesman to being an impartial and trusted partner.

If the objections start to flow at this point, do not engage in fighting each objection in an ever bloodier version of corporate trench warfare. Go back to step three: check that you both agree on the problem, then agree on the benefits of solving the problem. You need to create a problem-solving atmosphere, not a problem-generating atmosphere.

Next steps

Most people are not psychic: they will not know exactly what you want. You have to ask them for it. They expect you to ask: otherwise it will have been a pretty pointless meeting. But this is where many executives fail. They are too self-effacing to ask for the next steps. There are four simple ways of asking for the next steps that make it quite difficult for the other person to refuse:

1 **The direct close**: 'Can we buy the special widgets?'

2 **The alternative close**: 'Should we buy the widgets in one big order or split the order?'

3 **The assumed close**: 'So we are agreed that we are buying 100,000 yellow widgets.'

4 **The action close**: 'I will raise the widgets order and send it over to you.'

The weakest close is the direct one, because you invite people to say no. The sneakiest, and often most effective, is the alternative close. You are not giving them the option of saying no to the widget order: you are inviting them to choose only how they should be ordered. The assumed close is a power close because it takes quite a strong person to speak up, especially in a public meeting, and disagree.

At this stage, your preparation is often vital. Over the course of your meeting, you may discover that your plan A is not viable. If you have prepared properly, you will have a plan B and plan C, which will allow you to find a way forward rather than finding a dead end.

Summary of the PASSION principle

Preparation: understand what you want and what motivates the other person.

Alignment: build trust and rapport, make sure the other person is ready to talk.

Situation: make sure you both agree the problem, opportunity or exam question.

Size the prize: jointly agree the benefits of solving the problem you have agreed.

Idea: suggest your idea in the language of the other person.

Overcome objections: do not fight them, agree with them and work jointly to solve them.

Next steps: be clear about what happens next, be ready with your plan B.

3 Persuasion: two secret rules

The listening rule

All great persuaders and sales people share a common character-istic: they have two ears and one mouth. If you have this, then you are halfway to becoming very good at persuasion. Good influencers and leaders not only have two ears and one mouth, they also use them in that proportion. Persuasion is not about selling and telling. It is about listening well. If you listen twice as much as you talk, you are well on the way to success.

> If you listen twice as much as you talk, you are well on the way to success.

The partnership rule

Bosses and clients are used to acting as judges: they judge all the ideas coming before them. This is not a constructive relationship. Typically, it involves the plaintiff pitching his case with a stack of PowerPoint slides and memos to impress the judge. The judge then picks a few holes in the presentation to show she is smart and decides for or against the plaintiff.

A much better way is to turn the boss or client into a partner and a coach. Show that you are there to help with their problem or opportunity, not just to advance your own agenda. Throw away the PowerPoint slides. PowerPoint slides are the badge of shame that junior staff and sales people have to wear. Colleagues do not talk to each other over a stack of slides: they talk to each other over a cup of coffee. By throwing away the slides you:

● avoid getting locked into the logic flow of the slides

● can react flexibly to what colleagues are saying

- create the opportunity to listen and discuss like colleagues, rather than present like a plaintiff
- are forced to prepare very closely around the logical and emotional flow of the discussion you want to have
- avoid getting trapped into arguments about detail and data.

Do not worry about the data. Have a few killer facts in your mind. Then you can offer to send across the detail later.

If you listen really well, you can convince the other person that the big idea was theirs all along. You reinforce the useful things they say and ignore the unhelpful things. Do not argue if it is not necessary. Build agreement where possible. When you have enough agreement, summarise what they were saying and thank them for their insight. Your idea is now theirs and you have succeeded: no one argues against their own idea.

3.3 Coaching: no more training

In most sports there are players and there are coaches. Players play and coaches coach, but rarely do coaches play or players coach. There is a huge divide between the two. The best players rarely make the best coaches. The best coaches were often journeymen players.

In management, things are not quite so clear-cut, with unfortunate consequences. The good player (IT specialist, salesperson or trader) gets promoted and their natural instinct is to go on playing. Playing is what got them promoted and there seems little point in changing a winning formula. But formulas win only if conditions remain the same. Promotion changes everything.

The newly promoted player naturally wants to take on all the most challenging tasks. This is precisely the wrong approach. The role of the coach is not to make all the tackles and score all the goals for the team. The role of the coach is to help the team achieve all these things, to bring out the best in each individual and to organise members effectively. The more the coach tries to be the best player, the more the team learns dependency. They rely on the coach to do everything. The coach thinks this shows the team is weak, so redoubles already Herculean efforts to make up for the team's weaknesses. The coach is playing ever harder to achieve ever worse results with a team that becomes ever more dependent. Eventually, there is an explosion and the coach is fired or gives up in total exhaustion.

The hardest lesson to learn for the newly promoted manager is to move from playing to coaching. Coaching is important because it:

● helps your team members to develop their talents

● lightens your load and the load of your team members

● enables you to focus on the right activities, rather than firefighting.

Coaching, like persuasion, is about listening and asking smart questions. This is easier to say than to do. When a team member comes to you looking for advice, the overwhelming instinct is to give them the answer. As soon as you do that, you have become a player again and the team member has learned nothing except to depend on you even more. Giving the answer may be quick in the short term, but creates a dependent team long term that will suck out all your time and energy. If you help members discover the answer for themselves, you may also find that they have a better answer than the one you first thought of. At a minimum, they will feel more commitment to a solution they have created than one you have imposed on them.

There are many coaching models available. In essence, they all boil down to roughly the same five-step process. For alliterative purposes, we will arrange them into the five Os:

1 **O**bjectives.

2 **O**verview.

3 **O**ptions.

4 **O**bstacles.

5 **O**utcome.

At each stage, it is more important to know the right questions than to have the right answers. The coach brings a different perspective. This is fundamentally different from the idea of training, in which the trainer instructs people on exactly how to do something. The coach does not tell someone what to do. The coach helps each person discover what works for them. Trainers tell, coaches ask. Trainers have a set method that they enforce. Coaches can see things from different angles. Most managers default to the safety of training: 'Do it my way.' This is safe in the short term, but it fails to help each team member achieve their full potential.

1 Objectives

Step one is to understand the problem we are solving: this is the same logic as the persuasion model outlined above:

> What is it that you want to focus on, achieve, review today?

2 Overview

The next step is to gather all the facts, before forming a view or making a judgement. This takes some gentle probing, in which you encourage discussion of different perspectives. Do not get locked into the world-view of the person being coached: you have to help them see a broader perspective.

> Why is this important to you?
>
> What is the current situation?
>
> How do other people see this?
>
> How do you know they see it that way?
>
> What are the potential consequences, good or bad, of this?

3 Options

This is where you get them to take responsibility and control. Do not give them the answer, even if you think you have it. Let them discover the answer that will work for them.

> Let them discover the answer that will work for them.

Push them to think of more than one option. In very difficult situations, there may not be much they can control: urge them to find something they can control. The more people feel a sense of control over their destiny, the less anxious they will feel. Then get them to evaluate the options they have generated:

What choices do you have?

What can you control or influence?

Have you seen anyone face anything like this before? What did they do?

How would you evaluate the benefits, risks and consequences of each option?

As they evaluate each option, they will gravitate naturally towards one solution. If in doubt, back their solution not yours. You want them to be committed. They will be committed to making their idea work. If you impose your solution, they will be committed to showing it does not work.

4 Obstacles

This is your reality check. Ask simple questions:

What will prevent you doing this?

What support will you need?

What obstacles do you see?

If you fail to ask these questions, you run the risk that they will give up when things start to get tough. But, if you have both predicted the challenges, you will be better prepared for them and you will be able to keep going.

5 Outcome

Finally, check for understanding. The big risk here is that you both feel happy and confident, but have different understandings about what happens next. Do not ask if they understand: a mumbled yes often means not really. The best way to check for agreement is to ask them what they think happens next. They should say what you expect: if they say something different, you will have averted disaster by catching the misunderstanding early.

By now, you will have noticed some familiar themes running through both persuasion and coaching:

● Listening is more important than talking.

● Questions are at least as important as answers.

● Understand the question before offering the answer.

These may seem very obvious lessons. The reason for spelling them out is that very few managers consistently follow these principles. By following them, you will start to stand out from the crowd.

How to delegate: who, what, how, when and why

1 Be very clear about the desired outcome (what)

Be clear about the overall goal and what good looks like: specify in detail what you want. Confirm understanding by asking your team what they think you have asked them for.

2 Try to delegate everything (what)

Be clear about how you add value in your role: building and supporting your team and perhaps taking on one or two projects yourself. Everything else should be delegated.

3 Delegate interesting and challenging work (what)

Stretch your team and let them develop; trust them to grow and to deliver. Do not delegate just the routine rubbish and do not hog all the interesting stuff for yourself.

4 Never delegate responsibility or the blame (what)

You are always responsible for the outcomes of your team: if it goes wrong, shield your team from the blame and learn from the experience. Delegate your authority and empower and support your team.

5 Delegate to the right people (who)

You can delegate sideways to your peers and up to your boss. Do not be the lone hero who does it all; leadership is a team sport, so get the right help at the right time from the right people.

6 Watch for overload and for shirking (who)

Look for the signs of stress: irritability, sickness, lapses and errors, tiredness. Be ready to pull back and shift workloads. Move the shirkers off your team.

7 Be clear about deadlines, milestones and reporting (when)

Do not over-monitor: that shows lack of trust. Try MBWA: management by walking away. But have clear deliverables by clear dates so that you avoid unpleasant surprises and can take corrective action early.

8 Be flexible about the means (how)

Do not specify how the work should be done. Let the team decide: they may even come up with a better way than you had in mind.

9 Empower and support your team (how)

Set up your team for success; make sure they have all they need; deny them the chance to make excuses later. Check and ask them what they want and what obstacles they expect.

10 Be clear about why the goal is relevant (why)

Explain the context so your team understands what is important and where they should focus. Show the task is important, worthwhile and relevant so that they can engage with it fully.

3.4 Delegating: doing better by doing less

Many managers find it difficult to delegate. Common excuses include:

- This is too important to delegate.
- This is too urgent: I need to do it myself.
- The team is not strong enough yet, they are not ready.
- Only I have the skills to do this.
- The team already has too much to do.
- I cannot risk letting the team screw up on this one.

All these excuses come down to lack of trust in the team and an inflated sense of the manager's unique skill. And they all condemn the manager to becoming overworked and the team to becoming over-dependent on the manager. The team will grow only if the manager can delegate and trust it.

Delegating and coaching go hand in hand. They both ensure that managers achieve the core task of management: getting other people to do things. The process of delegation is simple.

1 Work out what you can delegate

In practice, there is very little you cannot delegate: evaluations, promotions, disciplinary procedures, resource allocation and team formation are all the preserve of the manager. Assume that everything else you can delegate. Many managers work on the opposite assumption: they delegate as an exception, not as a rule. You should find that you delegate a mixture of fairly routine administrative and maintenance activities, combined with a few more stretching and engaging initiatives.

2 Know your team

Think carefully about who is best for which tasks. Balance their current capabilities versus their ability to learn and grow by doing the task. If a person is 60 per cent ready, then trust them. This can be nerve-racking, as you see them struggle with stuff that would be easy for you, but that is the best way they will learn. Once they have learned, they become more productive and valuable members of your team. Balance out the workload across the team. Given the ambiguous nature of managerial work, it is very difficult to estimate workloads in advance. In practice, you know which team members are shirkers and which are heroes who never complain about workloads.

3 Set clear objectives

When briefing a team member you need to give clarity and certainty to four things:

1   The expected outcome.

2   When the outcome must be achieved.

3   The reasons behind the goals you have set.

4   Intermediate objectives that let both of you know if things are on track.

If your team understands why you are making a request, they will be in a much better position to respond to questions and challenges as they arise, instead of having to refer back to you.

4 Discuss the process

You can be clear about the goals, but you need to be flexible over the means.

This becomes a negotiation around several key topics:

> You can be clear about the goals, but you need to be flexible over the means.

- How many resources (people, skills, budget) will be available to the team?

- How much decision-making authority will it have?

- How often will it be necessary to report?
- What is the best approach to take?
- Who else needs to be involved?
- How can the manager help in removing roadblocks, dealing with the politics?

This may be more than one conversation. The objective of this step is partly to set the team up for success. Equally, discussion gives the team a sense of ownership over the process. It might even come up with a really smart way of tackling the task that you had not thought about before.

A huge trap here is vagueness. If a team member says, 'I hope to… I will try… I will look into it…', they are making vague promises, which mean nothing. Misunderstanding inevitably follows. Be very clear about who does what by when. Do not ask the team if they understand because they will say yes, even if they do not understand. Ask them to summarise who will do what when. This quickly reveals any misunderstandings, before it is too late.

5 Follow-up

Managers delegate, never abdicate, responsibility. You are still responsible for the final outcome. Three key elements of the follow-up are:

1   Be available to coach, as required.
2   Check up on progress formally and informally, as discussed with the team at the start of the task.
3   Recognise the team's contribution and success when it has completed the task.

Some managers try to steal the limelight at the end of a successful effort by their team. This demoralises the team and does not help the manager. The manager looks much better to his bosses if he can show that he can build and manage a great team, than if he pretends to do all the hard work as a one-man band.

How not to delegate

David was a manager from hell. He genuinely believed he was good at delegating because he delegated a lot. What this meant, in practice, was that he delegated all the rubbish. This would be a toxic mix of the routine stuff that anyone could do, plus a few projects that were known as hospital passes: they were so late or so badly messed up that the person receiving the project was more or less certain to land up in career hospital. The manager was, effectively, delegating all the blame. He was very good at this.

To really mess his team up, he would give vague instructions about what he wanted and then shout at people when they failed to read his mind properly and provide exactly what he wanted. His vagueness also allowed him to change his mind frequently, which led to endless late nights and frustration as the team reworked projects for him.

Because he never really trusted his teams, he would ask for constant updates. More time was spent updating him than doing the work. The lack of trust was corrosive of team spirit and used up all the team's time.

If, by some chance, a good result emerged from this method, David was very keen to make sure that everyone knew he was responsible for the outcomes. Setbacks were, invariably, the fault of his inadequate team. Eventually, this became a self-fulfilling statement. Anyone who was any good found another boss, another department or another company to work for. He was left with the weakest players, which reinforced his belief that he could trust no one with delegated work. The misery cycle was complete, and was broken only when David finally left the company.

3.5 Handling conflict: from FEAR to EAR

Conflict is the natural state for most organisations. The most intense conflict is not against rival organisations. Conflicts are largely invisible on a day-to-day basis for most managers: HR, IT and operations staff are too focused on dealing with their immediate functional challenges to worry about marketplace competition. The real competition is not external: it is internal.

The biggest threat to most managers is not a rival organisation: it is a rival manager who may be sitting at a desk near them.

In a well-run organisation, this conflict is healthy. Conflict is the way that the battle for resources and priorities in the organisation is decided. There is a limited pool of management time, money, resources and skills. There is a limited pot of potential promotions, bonuses and pay rises. Every department, function and business unit will have a different perspective on how that limited pot should be divided up. The inevitable consequence is rivalry and conflict between managers within an organisation.

This conflict can be productive. It forces managers to show that they have the best way of using the limited resources of the organisation. Occasionally, this competitive conflict becomes dysfunctional. Dysfunctional conflict comes in two flavours:

- cold wars
- hot wars.

Cold wars are basically political and are an essential reality of management. Hot wars tend to be emotional, flaring up in an instant. Neither side is likely to come out looking good. But there is a question of survival: handle it badly and you can become damaged goods in the organisation.

Starting a hot war

We were standing in the school corridor, surrounded by well-behaved children. It was a school in a tough area, achieving great results. My colleague dismissed it as old-fashioned. This was, perhaps, not the ideal moment to inform him that he was being arrogant and narrow-minded.

The reaction was spectacular. His eyes bulged. His face went crimson and the veins on his neck popped out. Spittle spewed from his mouth, as he shouted, 'I have never been so insulted in all my life.' He quickly got a good audience for his performance.

> At this stage, I wanted to reply, 'In that case, no one has been trying.' It would have been fun to watch his reaction, and I really did not care what he thought any more. He was now in full raging and ranting mode. I needed to decide fast what to do next...

Principle one: know which battles to fight

Sun Tzu, the Chinese philosopher, wrote *The Art of War* about 2,350 years ago. Perhaps his most useful insight was in knowing when to fight. He gave three rules for fighting:

1 **Only fight if the prize is worth fighting for**. Most corporate battles are over small things: save your ammunition and personal credibility for the big battles. On small things, it is often easier to do a trade: concede one point and gain another in return.

2 **Only fight if you know you are going to win**. On Wall Street, the saying goes: 'If you don't know who the fall guy is, you are.' The last thing you want is a good clean fight: you want a completely unfair fight where you are sure to win. This is not just about having the best arguments. It is about having all your allies lined up well in advance.

3 **Only fight if there is no other way of achieving your goal**. Enemies are not good for your career. Find a way of coopting people onto your agenda; align your goals with theirs; get an intermediary to broker a deal; do a trade with them over interests, timing, priorities or resources. To turn Clausewitz (a military philosopher) on his head: 'Diplomacy is a continuation of war by other means.' Diplomacy is the bloodless way of achieving your goals.

All three of these conditions need to be in place to make it worth fighting. But, when you do fight, fight hard. Remember the words of Colonel Tim Collins to his troops as he sent them into war during the second Iraq conflict: 'If you are ferocious in battle, remember to be magnanimous in victory.' You will need to win the peace as well as the war.

Principle two: from FEAR to EAR

Human instinct trumps human reason, especially at moments of stress and conflict. The natural reaction to danger is the flight or fight reaction, spurred on by a good deal of fear. In the context of your organisation, these are deeply unhelpful instincts. Running away or fighting the CEO at the first hint of a challenge could become a career limiting move. We have to find a way of managing our feelings.

Deciding whether to fight

As my colleague's arms and arguments got carried away, I had a chance to think through the rules of war:

1 Is there a prize worth fighting for? None, other than my own dignity: the looks from the children showed that neither my colleague nor I had much dignity left anyway.

2 Am I sure to win? Since I did not know what I was fighting for, this seemed unlikely. There was no clear winning strategy.

3 Is there another way of achieving my goal? Perhaps the goal had already been achieved: his complacency and cynicism had been challenged.

Fighting looked pointless. The only question was: what to do next? I was feeling offended by his insults to me. I did not want to argue back. I wanted to hit him. He was still ranting. I had a moment or two to gather myself...

The FEAR instinct can be summarised as:

Fight furiously

Engage enemy emotionally

Argue against all-comers

Retaliate, refute reason

Like flight and fight, the FEAR reaction is not helpful. It is, however, a potentially memorable way to spend your last day with an employer. The first step in overcoming the FEAR reaction is to recognise it. Once we

> **The first step in overcoming the FEAR reaction is to recognise it.**

recognise it, we can start to control it. In training sessions, we ask managers how they deal with the FEAR reaction. Some of the more original ways of managing personal stress include:

- Become a fly on the wall: watch yourself and decide on the best course of action from this out-of-body position.

- Imagine what the person you most admire would do in this situation, and try it.

- Imagine the other person as a baby throwing its toys out of the pram: it is hard to get angry with a baby in a tantrum.

- Imagine the other person wearing a tutu: becoming angry with a fat 50-year-old in a tutu is very difficult.

- Focus on breathing: breathe deeply and slowly, regain control of your body and emotions.

- Count to ten before replying. Give yourself time to think, avoid inflaming the discussion any more and let the other person's storm blow itself out.

- Go to your happy place: everyone has a place in their heads that is safe and secure. Go there, take stock and then proceed.

All these tricks help achieve the essential first three goals:

1 Regain personal control.
2 Buy time to think.
3 Let the storm blow itself out.

It is extraordinarily difficult to sustain anger for more than two minutes, although those two minutes can feel like an eternity.

The only way to sustain the anger is to give it some more fuel. Give the angry person no fuel, and they will run out of steam fast. Fuel comes in several forms, including:

- engaging with them emotionally
- justifying and defending your position, which will lead to them arguing even more intensely about why you are wrong
- using body language to show how angry, upset or dismissive you feel.

Stopping the war

There was nothing worth fighting for. The best thing to do was to get the frothing, foaming fury to calm down. So, I threw away the last of my pride and dignity and did the hardest thing of all: I apologised.

He then threw the apology back in my face. I was insulted. Perhaps I should have hit him after all. But I stayed in control and apologised again. He threw the apology back in my face again. He could not hear reason. He was so self-consumed in his anger he could not see beyond the red mist. I had to stay patient and ignore the invitations to justify myself and provoke more warfare. I was finding it very hard to stay restrained. After five attempts, he finally calmed down.

Now to win the peace...

It is better to win a friend than win an argument. Winning a friend is the best way to win the argument. A friend is more likely to listen to reason and compromise than an enemy. A simple way of doing this is to remove the F from FEAR. What remains is EAR, which is what you should be using. Listening is a far better way of gaining agreement than talking and persuading. EAR stands for:

Empathise

Agree the problem

Resolve the way forward

Empathise

Some people appear naturally empathetic. The rest of us have to learn the skill. Fortunately, it is quite easy. You do not have to become a fully qualified shrink, a neuro-linguistic programming expert or an agony aunt to become empathetic. Here are three simple ways in which you can become more empathetic in your dealings with colleagues:

1 **Stop talking at them**. Instead, let them hear the voice of perfect reason and harmony: their own voice. Do not feel the need to fill a silence. Let them fill the silence with their own wisdom. Listening is a wonderful way of letting opponents talk themselves into submission, buyers talk themselves into agreement and lovers talk themselves into bed.

> Listening is a wonderful way of letting buyers talk themselves into agreement and lovers talk themselves into bed.

2 **Listen actively**. Show that you are listening by paraphrasing back what you heard them say. Do not repeat what they said: this appears artificial. Show that you have absorbed what they said and have interpreted it. If you misinterpreted, they will tell you quickly and you avoid any misunderstanding. If you interpreted correctly, they will think that you are wonderful for hearing their wisdom so well.

3 **Ask open questions**. Open questions encourage people to talk more. A closed question encourages a yes/no answer, which kills the conversation and has the potential to create conflict if the answer is no. Open questions often start with a what, how or why. These are difficult to answer with a yes or no.

Agree the problem

Many conflicts are about different agendas and priorities. Finance is focused on cost control, and marketing is focused on revenue generation. The result can be a dialogue of the deaf. If the problem remains decreasing costs versus raising revenues, there is no rational discussion to be had. So the two sides need to agree a common way of looking at the challenge. In reality, both marketing and finance should want to increase the profitability of the organisation. Once both sides agree a common challenge, they can agree a common way forward: marketing investment needs to show an adequate return to shareholders. There is still plenty of discussion and debate, but at least both sides are now working towards the same goal and share the same language.

This is a stunningly obvious point, which is why it is normally missed. There is a real art form in changing the nature of the conflict from a win/lose to a win/win. Costs versus revenues is a win/lose argument. Increasing profitability can become a win/win for both sides.

Resolve the way forward

This rational discussion can happen only when both sides have got past the emotional problems of the hot war and when they have agreed the common problem. In practice, this is often the easiest part of the discussion. If you are jointly trying to find a way through, you are likely to succeed. If you are trying to fight your way past each other in opposite directions, you will find it difficult to make progress.

This is, hopefully, a rational discussion based on emotionally and politically stable foundations. Because it is a rational discussion, it is covered in detail in Chapter 2: Solving problems: prisons and frameworks – and tools.

By now you may have noticed that IQ, EQ and PQ have reared their ugly heads again. The EAR process of resolving a hot conflict pulls together the three core management skills:

1 EQ: empathise, remove the emotional heat of the moment.
2 PQ: agree the common problem, align agendas.
3 IQ: solve the problem and agree the way forward.

Importantly, deploy EQ, PQ and IQ in that order: EQ first and IQ last. Many managers start with IQ and land up having endless logical arguments that go round in circles. Deal with the person first, and the problem will melt away.

Winning the peace

After we had both calmed down, we realised we had both acted unwisely. Shame-faced, we made peace. As we did so, we realised quickly that we both shared the same ambition of helping achieve greatness in the most challenging urban schools. We realised we both saw many of the same opportunities and we disagreed only on detail. We could now make progress and win together: he is the best of allies anyone could ask for in such a tough task.

Of course, the real lesson has nothing to do with dealing with conflict. The real lesson is that it is much smarter to avoid creating the conflict in the first place. The art of giving feedback constructively is dealt with in the next section. Giving the wrong person the wrong feedback at the wrong time and in the wrong place was not smart.

3.6 Giving informal feedback: making the negative positive

Managing would be much easier if it did not involve people. At the heart of management is the idea of making things happen through other people. We need to get the best out of our team and our colleagues. This requires a fine balance of providing support and encouragement (positive feedback) and improving performance (constructive feedback). If that is the theory, the reality for many team members and managers is a combination of no feedback (instead of positive feedback) and negative feedback (instead of constructive feedback).

If nothing else, it is worth keeping in mind the perceived reality and the ideal to which we might aspire:

Perceived reality	Ideal
No feedback	Positive feedback
Negative feedback	Constructive feedback

Principle one: give positive feedback

Positive feedback is not simply about being nice to people. Positive feedback helps because it:

- encourages the right sort of behaviour
- builds the confidence of the recipient of the feedback
- opens up a non-threatening dialogue about performance, making coaching easier
- raises both individual and team morale.

There are good and bad ways of giving even positive feedback. Essentially, the principles are the same as when giving effective constructive feedback, outlined next.

Principle two: make constructive feedback constructive

Constructive feedback is the art of changing perspectives and behaviours. There are some tried and tested ways of doing this well and poorly. The four basic steps of giving constructive feedback are:

1 Find the right time and the right place.
2 Be specific, not general, and focus on behaviour not the person.
3 Pause.
4 Solve the problem and move to the next steps.

Find the right time and the right place

Constructive feedback requires a change in perspective or behaviour: that implies criticism of current behaviour. People do not like criticism, especially in public.

Give the feedback in private, not in public. Do not force someone to defend themselves in public or shame them in public: it will get a negative reaction.

Power of positive feedback

John Timpson owns a chain of shoe repair shops that bear his name. He set himself the goal of giving ten pieces of positive feedback for each piece of negative feedback. This has a powerful effect. It highlights and reinforces the sort of behaviour and values he wants to encourage. Praise sets the norm and quietly discourages inappropriate behaviour. By praising a shop worker who returns some money a customer has lost, he sets the standard: staff know that this is a company that encourages honesty and fair dealing. It is a more powerful way of communicating the message than putting in rule books, procedures and sanctions designed to punish the wrong sorts of behaviour. Praise builds a culture of commitment: rules build a culture of compliance.

Give the feedback near enough to the actual event for it to be fresh in the memory, but not if the person is still upset or angry about what has just happened. Let them calm down first: reassure them that you are not going to bite their head off. Then they may start to transition from an emotional state to a more rational state.

The clear difference with positive feedback is that often it is best given in public. People like public recognition, and it sends a signal to the rest of the team about the sorts of behaviours that you believe are important to the success of the team.

Be specific, not general, and focus on behaviour not the person

Telling someone that they are unprofessional is, in itself, unprofessional. It is very general and it is an attack on the person. It invites a fight rather than a change in behaviour. Take the concern and ask yourself why you made that judgement. Then focus on the specific behaviours that led to that comment. For instance, 'I noticed you have turned up late to work four days in a row,' is a factual description of behaviour. If they agree with this, you may be ready for the next step.

The same principle applies with positive feedback. Saying, 'I think you are a wonderful person,' is unhelpful: it is not actionable and probably sounds insincere. Saying, 'That solution you came up with on customer service was very creative, and it has worked,' is specific.

Choice of language is important here. Generalisations such as never, always and everyone are unlikely to be accurate and will inflame things.

Pause

Give the other person a chance to react. There are several ways of doing this:

- Shut up. There is no need to fill the air with your opinions. Give them space to respond.

- Ask an open question or invite a response: 'Lateness is not like you. I don't understand why it is suddenly happening.'

- Reflect on how it affects you personally: 'It has made life difficult for me because...' Use reflection as a prompt only if the first two options are not generating a response.

At this point, you may find they have a domestic crisis, or they have been working exceedingly late, or there may be some other reason that you can work on together. You are inviting the other person to become a partner in solving a joint problem, rather than being a boss that is going to scold a team member like a parent scolding a child. You are trying to construct an adult to adult conversation, not a parent to child script.

Do not move to the next stage unless you can:

- agree the problem, or at least the symptoms of a problem (e.g. lateness)

- agree that the problem needs to be solved: it is important and relevant

- agree the causes of the problem.

If you do not have these agreements in place, you may find the discussion going round in circles, from symptoms to causes to facts to solutions and who is to blame.

In this pause, let the other person reflect on why things are happening the way they are. Simply saying 'I never expect to see you late again' is unhelpful. You may be addressing the symptom of a problem (lateness) not its cause (domestic crises, late-night working, and disenchantment with work). Trying to remove the spots from a child's face with spot remover is not going to work if the child has measles: to cure the symptoms you have to cure the cause of the problem.

Solve the problem and move to the next steps

The trick here is to make it their solution: you want them to feel a sense of commitment to an idea that they own. If you have done the groundwork properly, you will now be able to go into coaching mode, rather than feedback mode. Follow the principles outlined in section 3.3: Coaching: no more training.

Questions, not answers, lie at the heart of good coaching. Let the other person discover the answer for themselves. If they discover the answer:

> Questions, not answers, lie at the heart of good coaching.

- they will be more committed to their answer than an answer you impose on them
- there is a risk that their answer may be better than the one you originally had in mind. It is a risk worth taking.

Constructive feedback: questions versus answers

I was ready for an ear bashing from the partner. I had not really delivered on a project. I knew and he knew, even if the client did not really know it. I went to his office and closed the door with my heart in my boots. It felt like going to see the head teacher on a detention. I was not looking forward to the interview.

▶

He then surprised me. He said, 'You are definitely one of our high-potential associates. Maybe one of the best.' He went on to describe the specific events that led him to that conclusion. Then, with just a hint of a wry smile, he asked, 'How did you feel about the last project?'

With very little coaxing I spilled the beans on how bad it was and why it was so bad. So he asked me how I would handle things in future. I knew what I wanted to do. We discussed various ideas and agreed a plan. He asked if I needed any help and we agreed to meet again in a couple of weeks to see how things were going.

I had gone into the room feeling bad, but I left feeling good. I knew what I had to do. I had a supportive boss.

After I left, I realised that he had never made any criticism and never offered any solution. He had just asked a few questions. I had done all the work for him. As I result, I owned the problem and the solution. I left the room committed to action, rather than feeling resentful about a ticking-off.

3.7 Using time effectively: activity versus achievement

Time is our most valuable resource. We have a limited amount of time, which ultimately runs out. We all have a use-by date in our careers and lives. There are only three ways in which we can make the most of this limited resource:

1 Delegate: get other people to do things and save our time for other matters.
2 Be efficient in what we do: do things the right way.
3 Be effective in what we do: do the right thing.

Delegation has already been covered in section 3.4: Delegating: doing better by doing less. If we cannot delegate well, then we will rapidly run out of time and we will fail the most basic test of management: we will be unable to make things happen through other people.

After delegating what we can, we are left with efficiency and effectiveness.

Time efficiency

Much of the modern world is obsessed with time efficiency: we want to do everything faster and to multi-task at the same time. We are desperately trying to squeeze a quart of activity into a pint pot of time. But there is a paradox here. The more we use the time- and labour-saving devices, the more stressed and time-starved we become. Technology does not free us: it enslaves us.

> Technology does not free us: it enslaves us.

There is a simple resolution of the time paradox. Time- and labour-saving devices never save time: they raise expectations.

Technology may save time, but for whom? It is always the employer, not the employee, who has to reap the benefits of increased productivity to stay competitive. Technology puts employees on a treadmill where we have to run faster and faster just to stay still. The faster we run, the faster our competitors run. We are running flat out, but we are standing still compared to our competitors. Standards rise, and employees pay the price.

Technology and the time paradox

Technology does not save time: it eats time by raising expectations.

Presentations

Old world: presentations were a slow and expensive nightmare, involving art departments and graphics people to prepare slides. As a result, each presentation tended to be short and concise.

New world: PowerPoint enables executives to prepare 200-page documents with lots of snazzy back-up slides without the time and expense of art and graphics departments.

▶

Result: executives waste time on PowerPoint, preparing presentations that are far too long. PowerPoint has raised expectations and no executive dares to be left behind. Labour has not been saved: standards have gone up.

Transport

Old world: the boat from England to Empire, or from Rome to Judea, took weeks and was very expensive. So, when people travelled, they made sure they got a serious result. And they also had to delegate. There was no time to ask for directions from Rome or London on how to handle a local riot: people on the ground had to be trained and trusted to make big decisions by themselves instead of setting up a global conference call to cover their backs in case it all went wrong.

New world: the one-day transatlantic visit is a badge of corporate honour to show how busy the executive is. It is also a sign that the local people are not seen to be able to do things by themselves.

Result: because we can travel more, we do travel more. More stress, more jet lag and more air miles.

Communication

Old world: letters written by hand or typed (with plenty of correction fluid) meant that there were few letters written, but that each one was important and commanded attention. Replies were slow but equally important.

New world: email and smart phones mean that we are meant to be in touch 24/7, even on holiday, with rapid responses to a deluge of trivial messages that are sent out on a just-in-case basis.

Result: email and smart phones increase the working week and stress. Information hyperinflation has made each message potentially worthless.

If technology will not save our time, we need to find some more, old-fashioned ways of maximising personal efficiency.

Do it right first time, every time

Rework is a time killer. It can more than double the time taken for a task. Rework means more than doing the work again. Unpicking work can be very time-consuming. It means trying to find out where things went wrong in the first place; renegotiating with people who were involved in the early work and trying to re-establish personal credibility and authority. To do it right first time means slowing down in order to speed up.

> ## To do it right first time means slowing down in order to speed up.

Slowing down is about planning work carefully at the start, negotiating and checking expectations with key stakeholders before starting and then checking progress at regular intervals to avoid misunderstandings later. Like the slow tortoise that moves purposefully forwards, you can beat the hare that runs in circles.

Handle each communication once

Half-doing a job is as bad as doing it wrong: both result in unnecessary rework. In the case of communications, unanswered phone calls and emails simply add to the mental logjam of stuff that clutters things up. It is an unwanted distraction. There are four ways of dealing with most communications: do it, delegate it, defer it or ditch it. In order of priority, they are:

- **Ditch it**. File in the number one file: the waste bin. Avoid getting sucked into fruitless activity by responding to the most insidious form of junk mail – email from colleagues who copy everyone in on everything. The waste bin is the busy executive's best friend.

- **Delegate it**. Push the communication back to the sender, or on to someone else, for action. Ensure the recipient knows why they are receiving the communication and what action they are expected to take.

- **Do it**. Most emails and phone calls can be dealt with immediately ('yes, I will forward that report to you; no, I cannot come to that meeting'). Use the three-minute rule: if you can do it in three minutes, do it and get it out of the way.

- **Defer it**. If more work is required, be clear about what will happen and by when. This then becomes an item to sort out in your overall priorities (time effectiveness is discussed below). As this is now an addition to your workload, the defer it option is the least attractive of the four options.

Some non-actionable items may contain useful information. Note it, file it and move on.

Do it now: avoid procrastination

Classic symptoms of procrastination are displacement activities. Instead of doing the job, people do something else like surfing the web, having a coffee, gossiping or doing a minor task. The causes of procrastination will be some combination of the following:

- **Wrong time of day**. Our energy levels go up and down over the day. Find easy tasks to do when your energy levels are low and tackle the harder stuff when your energy levels are up and when you are least likely to be distracted by other people and issues.

- **Job too difficult or ambiguous**. The hardest jobs are the easiest to delay. Break down a large job into bite-sized chunks so that you do not get indigestion even thinking about the problem. It is easier to see progress and feel motivated by tackling a series of small tasks than trying to tackle one huge problem. Like climbing a mountain, it is best done one small step at a time rather than attempting one big leap.

- **Perfectionism**. Waiting for the perfect conditions or the perfect outcome is as fruitless as *Waiting for Godot* (Samuel Beckett's play). The perfect is the enemy of the good. Find an acceptable start and end point. The important thing is to move to action and do what you can, rather than worry about what you cannot do. If you worry about what you cannot do or control, you will never stop worrying and never achieve anything.

- **Confusion**. Lack of clarity around goals and how to get there can lead to rabbit in the headlights syndrome: the executive is frozen. Ask for help and guidance from the boss: get out of the headlights before the deadlines run you over.

- **Chaos**. This comes in two versions. The first version is the physical chaos of papers strewn all over the desk: each person needs to find their own preferred working environment, but chaos is rarely effective. The second version of chaos is chaos around priorities, which leads straight back to the rabbit in the headlights syndrome.

Time effectiveness

Time-efficient managers can be spotted everywhere. They are at the airport, talking on their phone while writing emails on their laptops. They can be spotted bumping into people on the street as they play with their highly addictive smart phones. Whether they are achieving anything is another matter. Many executives make the fundamental mistake of confusing activity with achievement. At year end, however, it is achievement and not activity that counts for bonus and promotion.

> Time effectiveness is about doing the right things.

Time efficiency is about doing things the right way. Time effectiveness is about doing the right things. Being 100 per cent perfect at doing the wrong thing is still a 100 per cent waste of time. The real management challenge is to do the right things. Doing the right thing is a mixture of three elements:

1 Knowing what you want to achieve.

2 Focusing on the important stuff.

3 Dealing with the urgent stuff.

Charles Darwin: activity versus achievement

Charles Darwin had all the appearances of a leisured toff. Reading his account of the three-year voyage of the *Beagle* is a revelation. He did not spend most of his time at sea or in scientific pursuits. He spent most of his time on land, visiting friends of friends in places like Argentina and having a very agreeable time. He was, by modern standards, wasting his time completely.

But he was not completely idle. Famously, he collected and studied different varieties of finches in the Galapagos and was baffled by their slightly different beaks. He continued to think about this after his return to England. He was a geologist by training and thought only as a geologist can think: in the millions of years that enable the sea bed to rise into mountains. With that sort of time he could imagine how animals could adapt and change dramatically. Slowly, he formulated the idea of evolution.

Darwin may have been idle by modern standards, but he was also focused. Being focused, he achieved far more than all the stressed-out, multi-tasking 24/7 executives who are busy being important. Activity and achievement are very different concepts.

Knowing what you want to achieve

There are no simple answers, but there are some simple questions.

Not all of us will have the chance to transform one of the sciences. But, if we want to be effective with our time, we should think carefully about what we want to achieve. There are no simple answers, but there are some simple questions.

These are deeply irritating questions to be asked when the flak is flying. They are questions to think about at quiet moments away from the pressures of work.

- When (if) I retire, what will I tell my grandchildren I did?
- In 10 (20) years' time, how will I remember this year?

- What are my goals for this year? Quarter? Month? Week? Day? Hour? Now?
- Are my activities now consistent with my answers to the first three questions?
- How can I create or find a context that allows me to achieve what I want in the first three questions?

Here are some things you will not remember in 20 years' time:

- the number of emails sent, phone calls made or meetings attended
- your year-end bonus or pay rise
- your performance against your official targets
- time spent in the office or on the road.

These, however, are exactly the sorts of things that consume most management time and attention on a daily and annual basis. The point about them is that they are not ends in themselves: they are means to an end. Emails, meetings and phone calls are all essential activities, but they are relevant only if they lead to achieving something meaningful – both professionally and personally. Even beating this year's sales target is not an end in itself: it is a means to some other professional or personal goal. Personally, it pays the bills and may help fund some long-held desire; professionally, beating sales targets is, perhaps, just a stepping stone to getting that job or starting that organisation that you have always wanted.

Knowing what you want to do sounds obvious, but it is not. In George Orwell's words: 'To see what is in front of one's nose needs a constant struggle.' Many executives fail to see what is in front of their noses. Immediate challenges blind them to other opportunities. Occasionally, a sideways move to build experience, skills and networks offers a better way of achieving long-term goals than mindless focus on goals mandated from above. The courage to move sideways comes only from knowing what you are looking for.

Focusing on the important stuff

The typical management day is crammed with urgent items. The daily flood of emails and phone calls threatens to drown us if we do not deal with it. But the risk is that urgent matters crowd out important matters. The short term always takes priority over the long term. The problem with this approach is that, at some point, the long term becomes short term and what could have been handled easily suddenly becomes a crisis.

There are three simplistic solutions to this, which in some circumstances can work:

1 Deal first with matters that are both important and urgent. The problem with this is that not all important things are urgent. Aged 65, people discover pensions are important and urgent. At age 25 they may still be seen as important but they are not urgent, so they are ignored: welcome to an impoverished old age.

2 Set aside time in the day for important matters and allow no distraction from urgent matters. This is a solution favoured by time-management gurus who do not have to live the reality of management: shutting out the external world is not a viable option for many managers.

3 Delay working on matters that are not important. The problem is that even unimportant things need to happen. If you build a computer, ordering the high-value processors clearly is very important. Ordering the low-value Styrofoam packaging seems much less important – until you try shipping the computer without it. Just because something appears unimportant does not make it unnecessary. It still has to be done.

The problem with many important agenda items is that they are also the most complicated, most time-consuming and longest lead-time items. Often, it is not possible to deal with them by locking the door and shutting out urgent matters for an hour or two. The more practical answer is to break down the big task into smaller bite-sized tasks, as outlined above. Even if you cannot find two hours in the day to deal with important matters, you can find a few minutes in which to have a critical conversation with someone, to check a few facts or to ask for some advice. With important and difficult matters, thinking ahead pays big dividends. Work back from the desired end result and identify the critical path for getting there. This allows you to start things early and avoid time-consuming crises later. Start the analysis early; find out early what the approval mechanisms are; get advice, direction and support early; do some early tests. All of these things help shape and focus later work which will save time. It also means that when, inevitably, there is a setback it does not automatically become a crisis around deadlines. You have spare time and do not need to get stressed out.

Time management and the cookie jar

Try this experiment. Take a large cookie jar. Put some big stones in it until there is no more space.

No more space? Put in some small pebbles until there is no more space between the stones.

No more space? Try pouring in some sand around the pebbles, so that there really is no more space.

No more space? Pour in some water, until it is at the top of the cookie jar. Now it really is full.

Now think of your day. The large stones are the really important things you must achieve. Put them into your day first and work on them. In the spaces between your important stones, you can fit in a few things you really want to do (the pebbles). In between all the pebbles are the sand and the water: these are the small but irritating things you have to do anyway, like answering emails, which can be fitted into any small spare slots in the day.

Queues and delays were invented specially for dealing with emails and phone calls, which otherwise would get in the way of dealing with the important stones in your day. The cookie jar test is a simple way of making sure you deal with the important stuff, not just the urgent and routine stuff. You can as easily fill a cookie jar with sand and water as you can fill your day with urgent and routine stuff: do not let it take over and prevent you dealing with the important stuff.

Time management comes down to observing a few simple, practical, obvious and even boring disciplines:

- Create your personal list of long-term (five-year-plus) goals. Three goals at most: one goal is better. Then look long and hard at how you will get there and how well your current situation meets your needs. To avoid death by list mania, these are goals that often are best kept in your head.

- Create your list of goals for this year. A good list will have the following characteristics:

  - It will be short: perhaps three professional and three personal goals.

  - The professional goals should fit with what your boss expects: negotiate if you can.

  - Personal goals should align with your professional goals. Perhaps you want to acquire some skills or develop some new options from within your current work.

  - Goals are not just financial and numeric: they can be about skills, people, life and family events.

  - Test your annual goals against the 20-year rule: if I achieve these goals, will I remember this year in 20 years' time? If you forget a year, you have lost a year of your life.

- Create your list of goals for this month and this week. The weekly goals list is a quick exercise for Sunday evening. The weekly list will:

  - distinguish between important and urgent items, as described above

- support achievement of the monthly and annual goals

- break down the important items into bite-sized chunks that can be dealt with piecemeal over the course of the week.

- Create your to-do list for tomorrow. Do your best to schedule the day into three major chunks:

  - **Committed time**. These are, for example, obligatory meetings. Review them in advance to see how you can use them to progress your important agenda items. The formal meeting may not help, but it may create the opportunity for an informal conversation with a difficult-to-find colleague.

  - **Urgent matters**. This ensures that urgent items are not dropped and do not become crisis items. Find a time of day when you enjoy dealing with this sort of stuff. Often, first thing in the day is when people are freshest and can deal with matters fast.

  - **Important matters**. Think ahead. Buy time by getting a head start on long lead-time items. Do not worry about doing it all: focus on what you can do now, not on what you cannot do. Do not seek the perfect solution, seek to make progress. If you try to hit a hole in one, you will waste time. Get your putter out and hit the ball a few feet towards the flag, even if it is 450 yards away. You may need rather a lot of shots, but you will have got to the hole faster than the person on the tee who is still trying for the hole in one.

There is one more tip for time management: once you have made all your lists, act on them.

> Once you have made all your lists, act on them.

Dealing with the urgent stuff

Urgent stuff may be unimportant and irritating. No one needs that request from a senior manager for an urgent reworking of a standard report into some custom analysis that is nearly impossible to perform. But management reality is that if the urgent stuff is not dealt with, it rapidly becomes a crisis. Dealing with urgent stuff has already been dealt with, in effect, in the section on time efficiency. The key principles are:

- Do it right first time, every time.
- Handle each task once: complete it while you can by doing it, delegating it or ditching it. (Challenge whether the urgent custom analysis really needs to be fully customised: perhaps just one essential piece of information is needed.)
- Do it now: avoid procrastination.

3.8 Minding your mind: the management mindset

Personal EQ is not just about what you do: it is about how you are. EQ is not about following a script. Nor can you achieve EQ by checking off lots of boxes on a checklist. You have to move beyond aping the symptoms of EQ and discover the causes of EQ.

The way we act is defined by how we think. If we really want to change how we behave, then we have to change how we think. At first, this sounds slightly intimidating. It sounds like we are committing to years of therapy with a highly paid shrink. You can do this if you want, but it is not necessary. We all have the instincts of the best managers already: we do not have to change who we are, we simply have to become the best of who we are. That is a more enticing prospect: build on our strengths, and let any (very minor) weaknesses fade away.

Over the last three years, I have led original research which shows that the best managers share the same mindset. The results were consistent across industries and geographies. Here are the seven mindsets of management:

1 **High aspirations**: reach for the best, and beyond.
2 **Courage**: dare to deal with the difficult stuff, beyond your comfort zone.
3 **Resilience**: embrace adversity.

4 **Responsible**: always the master, never the victim.

5 **Positive**: believe in better.

6 **Collaborative**: work through others.

7 **Learn**: always grow professionally and personally.

When you look at that list, you will, reasonably, assume that you have all those mindsets. On a good day, we can all be like that. The difference is that the best managers are always like that, and they take each mindset to an extreme.

There is plenty of good news about these findings:

- Anyone can learn these mindsets, and become better at them.

- Mindset has a multiplier effect on your skills: you can execute other EQ skills far better with the right mindset.

- Because no one can see mindset, it is your invisible source of competitive advantage over your peers, which they will not know about or be able to copy.

- You do not have to master every mindset, or perfect any. Becoming slightly better at one or two makes a big difference. Like playing a sport or musical instrument, a little practice goes a long way.

This section will look briefly at what each mindset means, and how you can build your version of it.

1 High aspirations: reach for the best, and beyond

A good manager will be practical and focused. They will:

- improve performance
- deal with the here and now
- focus on what they can do.

There is nothing wrong with that. But the very best managers and leaders think differently. The table overleaf shows the difference:

Good manager mindset	Best leader mindset
Improve performance	Seek to change, dare to be different
Deal with the here and now: start from the beginning	Focus on building a future perfect: start at the end
Focus on what they can do	Focus on what must be done to achieve the mission

The critical difference is where the best leaders start. They do not do the obvious and practical thing, which is to start from today. They start with a vision of a future perfect, which they want to build, and then they work back from there. This means they are not constrained by what they think they can and cannot do. Instead, they work out what they must do, and then find ways to make it happen. There is an old story of a traveller in Ireland who asks for directions to Dublin and is told: 'If I was going there, I wouldn't start from here.' Too many managers are constrained by where they start, instead of focusing on where they need to get to.

> Too many managers are constrained by where they start, instead of focusing on where they need to get to.

2 Courage: dare to deal with the difficult stuff, beyond your comfort zone

It is not enough to dream the dream. You have to dare to act as well, otherwise your future perfect is just a pipe dream. Obviously, you do not need the physical courage of the kings of old who led their troops into battle. You need a different sort of courage. When leaders talk about courage, this is what they mean:

- Have difficult conversations about expectations and performance.
- Make difficult decisions about costs and teams.

- Step up, not back, in a crisis.
- Take responsibility for setbacks.
- Challenge the status quo, do not accept it.

The easy route is the path of least resistance but, if you take the easy path, you will never climb the mountain. You will meander in the foothills of management. Acquiring courage does not require taking insane risks. It is about slowly building up your risk tolerance and risk awareness by regularly pushing yourself slightly outside your comfort zone. As your comfort zone grows, you slowly take on more risk. Eventually, you will be doing things that look very courageous to other people, but that will be second nature to you.

3 Resilience: embrace adversity

Courage is about taking risks. Not every risk can work out. By definition, some risks must go sour on you. In the words of the poet William Blake: 'You never know what is enough unless you know what is more than enough.' Risk means pushing yourself until you discover what is more than enough.

There are two sorts of resilience that managers need to build: short-term and long-term.

Short-term resilience is the ability to bounce back from setbacks. The best leaders seem not to understand the word failure. They may talk about the occasional setback, which simply means that they have not succeeded… yet. Keep in mind the mantra, 'I have not succeeded… yet'. That will drive you to the right short-term response to setbacks, which is:

- Focus on the future.
- Drive to action.
- Use each setback to learn and grow stronger.

Long-term resilience is about sustaining your energy and passion for a 40- or 50-year career. Fundamentally, that requires two things:

- **Enjoy what you do.** You excel only at what you enjoy. Enjoyment does not mean having fun: it means being so absorbed in what you do that you forget time. If each hour of the day stretches to eternity, you are probably not enjoying what you do. Only when you enjoy your work can you find the stamina to keep on going the extra mile to make things happen.

- **Have a meaningful mission or goal.** Various saints and martyrs down through the centuries have shown how far people will push themselves in pursuit of a cause in which they believe. If your goal is to meet some of your key performance indicators (KPIs) next year, you are unlikely to make the same level of commitment as the saints. The greater your mission, the greater your commitment.

4 Responsible: always the master, never the victim

Taking responsibility is a self-evident mindset. But the way the best leaders take responsibility is different from how most managers think about responsibility. You can see the responsibility difference in three areas: successes, failures and feelings.

- **Successes.** There are few managers who do not like taking responsibility for success. Everyone needs a claim to fame, and that means you have to stake your claim when you succeed. But the best leaders do something unexpected: instead of hogging success, they share it generously. They make sure that anyone who contributed to the success is recognised. This does two things. First, it helps create a loyal team and network around you: reciprocity is part of human nature and you will find you reap a good harvest for your generosity. Second, by giving praise, you identify yourself as the person who was at the centre of the success. Far from losing your claim to fame, sharing the success is an effective way of staking your claim.

- **Failures**. No one likes wearing the office equivalent of the dunce's cap. So, when you stand up and take ownership of a setback, the whole organisation breathes a quiet sigh of relief. Instead of playing the blame game, the organisation can focus on how to move forward from the setback, and you can turn disaster into triumph. When it comes to assessment time, most bosses will recognise that you behaved well. And, if you were at fault, bosses look far more kindly on team members who recognise the problem than those who go into denial: by recognising the problem, you show you can learn from it and improve.

- **Feelings**. Taking responsibility for your own feelings is one of the hardest lessons for managers. Imagine you have had a bad day at the office and then a colleague comes along and decides to wind you up: they know exactly which buttons to press to get a reaction. You have every right to feel angry and upset. But there is no law that says you must feel angry and upset: you can choose how you want to feel and how you want to react. As a manager, you will not be remembered for what you did: you will be remembered by colleagues for how you were and how you behaved. Once you know this, you can make an informed choice about how you want to react. Choose well.

5 Positive: believe in better

Being positive does not come from training sessions where you learn to say, 'Have a nice day.' Being positive comes from the heart. Research from the positive psychology movement shows that people with a positive outlook live longer and better, by a large margin.

> People with a positive outlook live longer and better, by a large margin.

It also shows that positive sales people outperform the rest by nearly double. For a manager, being positive is about some simple routines:

- Focus on the future, not the past. This means driving to action, not to analysis.

- Focus on what you can do, not on what you cannot do. Do not worry about what you cannot control.
- Find opportunities to praise, not to criticise.
- Look for opportunities, not problems. See the upside of an idea before assessing all the drawbacks. The biggest and best ideas often have the biggest drawbacks: do not kill them before you have found out how good the idea could be.

As a simple but dangerous exercise, recall every setback you have had today, from missed traffic lights to annoying emails. You may quickly feel quite gloomy about your day. Now recall every good thing that has happened, from waking up in a warm bed with access to clean hot and cold water. You should feel better. We can choose how we want to see the world, and how we see it affects how we feel. Your choice.

You can train yourself to think positively. One particularly positive and enthusiastic manager had an odd habit: she wore a rubber band where others might wear a bracelet. She always wore her rubber band. When challenged on this habit, she explained: 'Every time I have a negative thought, am about to criticise, be negative or say things cannot be done, I just snap the rubber band against my wrist. It reminds me that I can think differently. I can be positive. When I first wore the rubber band, I had a very sore wrist within an hour. Now I realise that being negative and cynical is just a waste of time. I do things differently now, and people treat me better as a result.'

Positive... about arson?

The head teacher reflected on what had happened in her first year in charge. On arrival, she found that the students spoke 68 different mother tongues. Many were first-generation immigrants, with all the attendant problems of poverty, integration and lack of employment.

'Of course,' she said, 'that is wonderful news. There is so much buzz and excitement from having such a diverse student population.

And first-generation immigrants show real commitment to wanting to learn and make their mark in their new community. They are a joy to teach.

'We had a challenge when one wing of the school was burned down by an arsonist. But that was a blessing in disguise. It released insurance money for redevelopment: that wing was getting old anyway.'

Most people would run away from such a challenging school. Where others saw problems, she saw only opportunities. Her confidence transmitted itself to staff and pupils and was reflected in both performance and appearance. She was so positive about the school wing being burned down I began to wonder who the arsonist had really been.

6 Collaborative: work through others

To be a manager is to make the vital transition from how to who. A team member, when faced with a task, has to ask: 'How do I do this?' The job of a manager is to make things happen through other people so, instead of asking how you have to ask, 'Who can do this?'

The importance of collaboration is growing as fast as the world of command and control is withering. Collaboration is not about telling people what to do: it is about using influence to persuade people who you do not control to work with you and help you. The art of influence and persuasion has been covered fully in section 3.2: Persuading people: how to sell anything.

The main features of the collaborative mindset are:

- move from how to who
- influence and persuade, not command and control
- build influence by building trust: align interests, do as you say and earn credibility
- give and take: support others when they need it
- listen, respect and share praise.

The collaborative mindset is hard. We all have our own window on reality: this tells us what is important for us and what we must do. The collaborative mindset recognises that there are many different windows on reality, and none is perfect. We have to understand and respect other people's reality. Only when we understand can we influence, persuade and change their minds. Understanding is not about agreeing with others: it is about laying the groundwork for effective influence and collaboration.

7 Learn: always grow professionally and personally

A career is a marathon, not a sprint.

A career is a marathon, not a sprint.

The work you do and the skills you need will change fundamentally over the course of a 40-year career. Looking back to a golden past may be fine when it comes to your taste in music or films, but is a disaster in terms of skills. Your job security does not come from your employer: in a world of technology change, globalisation and competition loyalty between employer and employee is a one-way street. You are expected to be 100 per cent loyal until you are no longer needed. Your job security comes from your skills, track record and a strong network, which can guide you to your next opportunity.

You have to keep your skills up to date. The skills you need change at each level of the organisation, as outlined in section 3.10: Learning the right behaviours: what your team really wants. Using the same skills in a different context does not work: you have to learn and grow.

Skills mastery is not just about training. Most training delivers know-what skills, which are useful but they are a commodity: accounting, law, IT are good skills, but there are plenty of people in other countries who will deliver the same skills at much lower cost. The skills that set the best managers apart from the rest are know-how skills. These are tacit skills about how you deal with people, how you make things happen, how you manage your boss, how much risk you take. There is no manual for this: you have to discover the rules of survival and success for yourself. Those rules change, depending on where you work. For instance, government and investment banking have very different risk appetites, working hours and styles: what works in one place will not work in another.

A simple way to keep on learning is to keep on asking two questions: WWW and EBI.

WWW means what went well. Ask yourself this question after every important meeting, call or event. The idea is to catch yourself succeeding. Most of us take success for granted. We assume that is how the world is meant to be. But reality is different: success is very hard to come by consistently. There are endless reasons why things go awry. And we cannot assume that our innate genius will put things right automatically. So, when things go well, reflect on why they went well and what you did to make it go well. The more you catch yourself succeeding, the more you will understand how and why you succeed. You will start to create your own success manual.

WWW is equally important when things do not work out quite how you expected. Even when things go wrong, there are probably some things you did well that averted an even greater setback. Again, catch yourself doing well and build your know-how and confidence.

EBI stands for even better if... Again, after any important event, ask what you could have done differently to get an even better outcome. The common alternative to EBI is WWW's evil twin: what went wrong. Post-mortem discussions are occasionally useful, and many of our most vivid lessons come from messing up: as children, we learn the danger of fire from touching something hot, and then we do not make the same mistake again. But, to focus on the negative is a good way to lose confidence and to start the dreaded blame game in your team. If you focus on how to improve, you will improve. You can use WWW and EBI as a good way to debrief with your team. You can also use it in quiet moments by yourself. You will find that, even walking down the corridor, waiting for a train or while having a cup of coffee, you can make such downtime productive by reflecting on the day and asking WWW and EBI. Do this and you can coach yourself to success on your terms.

3.9 Finding your performance zone: learn to thrive

Think for a moment about which sort of conditions bring out the best in you:

- **The chill-out environment**: undemanding work and deadlines; creative zones with funky chairs and whale music; and an understanding employer who provides generous holidays, team-building events, celebrations and concierge services. Nice place to work.

- **The work-out environment**: demanding work and deadlines; demanding but supportive bosses and colleagues; constant challenge and struggle with limited resources. Life beyond the comfort zone.

- **The stress-out environment**: demanding work and deadlines; unforgiving bosses; lack of control over your destiny; culture of fear and blame; little teamwork.

The work-out environment will bring out the best in most people. Most people will be stretched, without being broken. This is the ideal performance zone. The problem with stress is, when you go into overload, you will break down (illustrated in the zone diagram opposite). At this stage, the remedy is not to go back to the performance zone: you need to rebuild confidence in the comfort zone again before starting to stretch. It pays to recognise this and act accordingly, both with yourself and with your team.

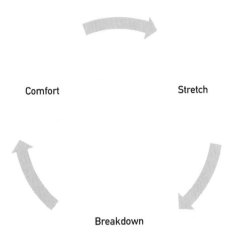

Comfort   Stretch

Breakdown

The zone diagram

At first, it seems odd that people put themselves into positions where they are going to be outside their comfort zones and put themselves under pressure. A cursory glance at the top graduate employers in most countries shows that the most popular employers are also the ones that generate the greatest amount of pressure: banks and consulting firms lead the way. Far from avoiding pressure, top graduates actively seek out high-pressure environments. After interviewing several hundred graduates for an hour each, some patterns become clear in this behaviour. Graduates seek the high-pressure employers because they:

- enjoy the prestige of being with what is perceived to be a top firm – they gain bragging rights with family and friends
- want to work with a peer group of equals, even though that means competition for promotion is far more intense than elsewhere
- want to gain experience that will help them build their careers longer term
- are slightly naive about the real scale of the challenge they face
- enjoy the buzz of a dynamic and exciting organisation and peer group.

You do not have to be an adrenalin junkie to want to work in a high-performing organisation with high-performing peers. Pressure is simply a by-product of such a desire. Highly demanding jobs are not the preserve only of banks and consulting firms: teaching in challenging inner-city schools (Teach First and Teach for America), becoming a junior hospital doctor or signing up for the armed forces all provide highly demanding environments that are very attractive to top graduates. Top managers do not avoid pressure or seek to minimise it: they actively seek out demanding situations that are personally rewarding.

Ultimately, people go into demanding situations because they enjoy them. This is smart thinking. You excel only at what you enjoy. No leading sportsman dislikes his sport, even though he suffers setbacks and losses. Equally, no successful manager dislikes her business, even though she too suffers setbacks and losses. The right amount of pressure helps people reach out of their comfort zone to improve their performance. Pressure, in the right amount, should be embraced, not avoided.

> Pressure, in the right amount, should be embraced, not avoided.

Walking, running and dying

Sarah had been poached from a rival electronics retailer. She would be a good source of competitive intelligence, so I decided to debrief her on her experiences.

JO: 'What is the biggest difference between this organisation and your last one?'

SARAH: 'People walk here.'

JO: '???'

SARAH: 'At my last place, no one walked. We never had time. We ran to meetings. If we heard the phone ring, we ran to pick it up within three rings. It was a constant rush. Very demanding, but with a real buzz.'

> JO: 'And here?'
>
> SARAH: 'We walk. People let the phone ring unanswered. It does not bother them. There is plenty of time for everything. I have moved from a running organisation to a walking organisation. It is much easier here.'
>
> Within three years, the walking organisation was out of business: outrun and overtaken by the running organisation. My next assignment was neither a running nor a walking organisation: it was a sleeping organisation. Being part of government, it is still in business.

We will look briefly at the nature of each zone: what it looks like and how you can use it to help you.

The comfort zone

Being told you are in your comfort zone usually is an insult, not a compliment. But your comfort zone has its uses, and there are times when you should operate in your comfort zone.

You know you are in your comfort zone when you find it easy to perform all your duties. You feel little pressure or stress, and you discover that work–life balance means you can have a life outside work. The good news is that, probably, you will perform well when inside your performance zone. You will be playing to your existing strengths.

Life in the comfort zone is important after experiencing a period of stress. You need time to recover, rebuild your confidence and recharge your batteries.

In the short term, life in the comfort zone is attractive, easy and productive: you will be seen to perform well. This is why the comfort zone is so dangerous: it is easy to be seduced into living there all the time. In the long term, this has serious consequences.

If you are in your comfort zone, you are not stretching yourself. You are not learning new skills that can help you in your next job.

You are quietly side-lining yourself. If you have an area of deep expertise, such as in law or accounting, this may let you sustain your career. But it will be a career limited to being a technical expert, not being a manager or leader. I hear many experts who eventually get very frustrated with their increasingly narrow expertise. One marketing manager, who was an expert in on-pack promotions, eventually gave up: he could not face doing yet another on-pack promotion for yet another brand. Boredom with routine had taken all the interest out of his job. He became a psychotherapist instead.

If you are becoming slightly bored with your routine, your career is not moving forwards and you are being marginalized, then, probably, you have spent too long in your comfort zone.

The stress zone

At the opposite end of the spectrum from the comfort zone is the stress zone. The checklist below shows the main symptoms of life in the stress zone.

Checklist of excessive stress

The major symptoms of excessive stress include:

- increased irritability: short fuse
- lower levels of physical and emotional energy
- increased frustration with the job and with colleagues
- more negative thinking: sense of the impossible, not the possible
- obstacles loom large – molehills become mountains
- feeling of being overloaded and out of control
- increased use of alcohol, tobacco, caffeine and drugs
- increased weight
- decreasing amounts of exercise
- poor and disrupted sleep patterns.

Be careful when you look at the list: it is like reading a medical dictionary and discovering that you have the symptoms of every single disease known to man. Hypochondria and paranoia quickly follow. Most managers will experience most of these symptoms at some stage: that is normal. When these symptoms persist or become acute, a death spiral starts: increased stress leads to worse performance, which leads to more stress, which leads to even worse performance.

Given that stress will happen for some periods in your career, it pays to know how to handle it.

The starting point is to recognise that the critical difference between pressure and stress is control.

If you are under pressure, you may work hard but you are also likely to thrive. Now apply the same amount of pressure and remove some of your control: your deadline is moved; you depend on critical inputs from others who may or may not deliver and you do not control; requirements and expectations keep on changing; different powerful people start demanding different things and you cannot reconcile competing and contradictory demands. Suddenly, the pressure turns to stress: the stakes are high and you have to deliver, but it is not clear what you must deliver, when or if you can deliver.

The main solutions are to regain control of the situation and of yourself.

Regain control of the situation

Step one is to review your situation. Clarify expectations about what is needed by whom and when. This may lead to some difficult conversations with bosses about what is, and is not, feasible. You do not want to be seen to be giving up on tasks. Instead, use these conversations to gain clarity around three things:

● **Priorities**. What needs to be done for whom and when. Be realistic: make sure that timings are achievable and work out what, if anything, can be pushed back or if requirements can be changed to make existing delivery dates feasible.

- **Resources, support and help**. Do not try to be a lone hero. If you need more support, be clear about what you need and when you need it.

- **Obstacles and dependencies**. If there are any obstacles to success, raise them now. If you depend on someone else to make it happen, and you are not sure they will deliver, raise the issue early. Deal with the challenge now, do not make excuses later.

Many people feel uncomfortable having these difficult conversations, which they see as a sign of weakness. Do not personalise the issue that way. The issue is not about you; it is about the nature of the work you face. Treat it as a business discussion about business issues and priorities. Have these discussions as early as possible: the earlier you have the discussion, the more actionable they become. If you leave it until the last moment, then there is little anyone can do to help you. Better to have a difficult discussion early, than to make excuses later.

> Better to have a difficult discussion early, than to make excuses later.

Step two is to review what you can do in the situation. Review the current challenges and assign them an ABC ranking:

A Important items that you can do something about. You may not be able to address the entire item, but there are a few things you can start to make progress on. Finding the early wins, building a little momentum, can quickly restore confidence both personally and with your colleagues. Focus on the few things you can do, not on the many things you cannot do.

B Items that are important and where you need help. The help may be in clearing a political logjam, clarifying goals, reordering priorities. Do not let the confusion and anxiety build up. Be proactive and seek a resolution. This is part of your conversation with your boss.

C Items that are less important that I can ditch, delay or delegate. Be ruthless in eliminating as much noise and junk from your to-do list: probably, you will need to focus all your energies on the A-list items.

The ABC approach is about gaining control, moving to action and rebuilding confidence. It requires focus on the things you can do (even if there are not many of them) and getting help on items where you do not have control.

Regain control of yourself

You have three strategies here, which you can combine: rest, relax, review.

Rest

Rest is tough in the heat of battle. But that is when you need a clear head most. If you pull an all-night working session, you may think you are a hero; if you pull an all-night drinking session, you may expect to get fired. But research shows that the effects of too much alcohol and too little sleep are exactly the same in terms of impaired cognition.

Sleeping in Brussels

Thursday was D Day: we had to pitch a big new idea to the board. At 8 pm, the presentation looked good, so I went to the hotel and slept. The team was really dedicated: team members stayed up until 2 am working and reworking the presentation. At 6.30 am they were back in the war room again.

At 7.30 am I rolled up. I nearly felt guilty that the team members had decided to stay up, even though I had encouraged them to get a good night's sleep. Their faces were white with exhaustion. I felt pretty good. They asked if they could now produce the presentation that they had revised overnight. I looked at it. It had gone backwards steadily from 8 pm the previous evening. The fine-tuning added lots of clever detail,

> but destroyed the logic flow and simplicity of the original. I let them produce the presentation: the 8 pm version. They were devastated.
>
> At 10 am, we presented. The pitch was simple, and it was familiar. The client loved it and we landed up working there for another 18 months. Doing less (well) is better than doing more (poorly).

The more fundamental approach to rest is to take time off work: have a real holiday where you dare to remove the shackles of email and smart phone. Even on holiday, it is easy to spot the hyped-up manager who is still in command, control and compete mode. Symptoms of the unrelaxed manager on holiday include:

- urgently organising friends and family, even though they would organise themselves quite happily
- barking demands and complaints at hapless receptionists, waiters and check-in staff
- itching to get back on to email and the smart phone, just in case something is happening back at the office
- boasting to all who will listen about their exotic travels, demanding work and high-maintenance lifestyle.

The world will not collapse if you are not holding it up for two weeks. If time off is as scarce as hen's teeth, then find a way of adjusting your assignments so you can revert to your comfort zone. If you stress out for too long, you will burn out and give up.

Relax

When the tension rises, our bodies change. Try this exercise: be angry while smiling and sitting back in your chair. It is more or less impossible. You can use this to your advantage: your mood is affected strongly by your body. If you are tensed up, with clenched fists, sweaty palms and bulging veins in your neck, then you are only a trigger hair away from a conflict.

Control your body and you control your mood. So, when the heat starts to rise, take action. There are many ways of learning to relax your body. Buddhist monks use meditation and breathing exercises. But you probably do not want to adopt the lotus position in the board room. Instead, you can at least learn to breathe in and out deeply a few times: let the fresh air come in and then you can breathe out all your tension. All it takes is a few breaths to make a difference.

You can also learn discrete airline-style exercises: from wiggling your toes, stretching your calves, unclenching your fist through to relaxing your shoulders. By the time you have relaxed your body, you will have relaxed your mind and you will be able to think more clearly and perform much better.

Review

After the event, take stock. Use WWW (what went well) and EBI (even better if...) to understand how you handled the situation and how you handled yourself. The temptation is to blame all our misfortunes on an evil world: bad bosses, idle colleagues, dishonest peers. That way we learn nothing and condemn ourselves to repeating our errors. Difficult times are when we can learn our most vivid and valuable lessons. Do not let such an opportunity go to waste.

The performance zone

Sports people often talk about being in the zone. Suddenly, everything goes right. For baseball sluggers and cricket batsmen, the ball suddenly looks like a slow-moving melon wanting to be hit, not a vicious speeding curving ball of menace. When they hit the zone, everything looks easy, even though it is based on years of painful practice. It is hard to stay in the zone for long: form comes and goes.

> We need to find ways of sustaining the performance zone for decades, not days.

In business, we all have moments like that, and they are equally temporary. In business, we need to find ways of sustaining the performance zone for decades, not days. You will know you are in the performance zone when:

- **time flies**: you are so absorbed in your role that you do not notice how fast time passes. You may realise in mid-afternoon that you have missed lunch

- **you are stretched**: you will be on the edge of what you think you can achieve. It will not look impossible (that is the stress zone), but you are pushing yourself to succeed

- **you are doing new things**: you are having to learn as you go, and you are probably excited about doing so.

This is the sweet spot between relaxing in your comfort zone and breaking down in the stress zone. In practice, you have to push yourself into this zone. Most HR systems will inadvertently push you back into your comfort zone: assignments tend to go to people who already have the relevant expertise. That means you learn nothing. The reality of work pressures means that many times you will be required to leap straight from your comfort zone to the stress zone without stopping to say hello to the performance zone.

Instead, you have to manage your career. If you are in the comfort zone, start volunteering discretionary effort for things that you know will push you; seek out assignments that you know will stretch you. Do not wait until you are 100 per cent ready to take on a big new role, because no one is ever 100 per cent ready for a big new role. Go for it early, and be prepared to learn fast on the job. Have confidence and belief in your ability to learn and grow.

If you are in the stress zone, have the difficult conversations early to reset expectations and to get the help you need.

Inevitably, you will swing between zones over the course of a year, let alone a career. That is fine. Do not expect to be in the performance zone the whole time. Manage yourself so that you achieve a balance between the three zones. That way, you can learn, grow and perform without getting side-lined in the comfort zone or burnt out in the stress zone.

3.10 Learning the right behaviours: what your team really wants

Read the literature carefully and you will discover that the ideal manager has the following characteristics and behaviours:

- ambitious and humble
- empowering and directing
- supporting and controlling
- task-focused and people-focused
- capable of seeing the big picture and the details
- intuitive and logical
- goal-centred and process-sensitive
- analytically rigorous and emotionally in touch
- entrepreneurial and reliable
- fast-moving and methodical.

Some managers feel they already have all these qualities and many more besides. They are arrogant and dumb enough not to feel the need to read this or any other book that might make them more effective. The rest of us feel small when measured against such demanding and contradictory criteria.

At this point, it makes sense to ask what managers expect of their peers, bosses and team members. Here are the results of a survey on the issue, with the criteria ranked by order of importance. The figures in parentheses are the percentage of managers who are satisfied with the performance of their peers against the chosen criteria.

Top leaders	Leaders in the middle	Recent graduates/ emerging leaders
Vision (61%)	Ability to motivate others (43%)	Hard work (64%)
Ability to motivate others (37%)	Decisiveness (54%)	Proactivity (57%)
Decisiveness (47%)	Industry experience (70%)	Intelligence (63%)
Ability to handle crises (56%)	Networking ability (57%)	Reliability (61%)
Honesty and integrity (48%)	Delegation (43%)	Ambition (64%)

Take a moment to review the list. Four key themes emerged from the survey:

1 The rules of survival and success change at each level of an organisation. This helps explain why people can succeed at one level and fail at the next. They have not become ineffective suddenly; they have found that a tried and tested success formula at one level does not work at the next.

2 Charisma and inspiration are notably absent from the list. This is a good thing. You cannot learn charisma or have a charisma transplant. They are not necessary. In the thousands of managers interviewed or surveyed, we found many effective individuals but few, if any, were truly charismatic. Managerial effectiveness does not require charismatic inspirational skills.

3 The expectations are additive: senior managers are expected to have all the qualities of new, middle and senior managers. They cannot abandon intelligence, hard work or reliability as soon as they are promoted into middle management. The performance bar rises at each level of the organisation.

4 Satisfaction with managers against the criteria outlined above is, at best, average. As mentioned, satisfaction levels are indicated by the percentages in brackets after each criterion. This is very good news for managers. It means that, by acquiring the skills and behaviours outlined above, they can stand out from their peers.

Your team will expect you to deliver on the expectations of a top leader, whatever your current level may be. As far as your team is concerned, you are the top leader. You need to act that way. Given that, it is worth briefly recapping what you need to do to become the leader your team wants to follow.

Vision

You need a simple idea of how the future will look different and better. This is more than just setting a stretching target. Show how the team will work differently: quality, customer focus, professionalism, zero defects, as the case may be. Then construct your story in three parts:

1 This is where we are, and this is why we need to change.
2 This is where we are going, and this is why the future perfect will be better.
3 This is how we will get there, and this is your vital role in helping us get there.

This story is vital to you. It gives purpose and direction to your team. Make the story personal to each team member: show how they can make a difference and how they can benefit from your future perfect world. The more relevant it is to each team member, the more committed they will be.

Ability to motivate others

When team members say they want a leader who can motivate others, what they really mean is they want a leader who can motivate them. And teams tend to be unimpressed with the efforts of their boss to motivate them: only 37 per cent of team members think their boss does well at motivation. You will be the last person to hear that truth from your team.

A whole industry devotes itself to understanding and promoting motivation, which goes all the way from abseiling away days to neuro-science. For our purposes, there is just one thing you can do to help. In our research we found that one question consistently predicted whether a boss would be rated well, not just on motivation, but also on most other dimensions as well. Here it is:

My boss cares for me and my career (agree/disagree).

If you pass this test, it is likely you are seen as good on motivation, decisiveness, vision, teamwork and all the other metrics. If you struggle on this metric, you will also struggle on the others.

Like all good insights, it is obvious when it is pointed out. If we have a boss who clearly does not care for us at all, it is very dispiriting. But a boss who seems to care makes all the difference.

Caring does not mean being nice and seeking popularity. Caring means that you should know what each team member wants and needs, you can give them the right roles, you support them and, where necessary, you have difficult but constructive conversations about performance with them. Care is about building trust, not popularity.

> Care is about building trust, not popularity.

Decisiveness

Decisiveness has been covered before under IQ. For a team, decisiveness is about clarity. Followership is, essentially, lazy: we want to know where we are going and how we will get there. The last thing we want is uncertainty and changes of direction, which lead to rework, lost time and missed deadlines. Often, any decision is better than no decision: you create a sense of direction and purpose and remove doubt and ambiguity. If you have doubts, be wary of sharing them with your team: you will look weak and uncertain. Your little doubts can grow into a major crisis of confidence within your team. Instead of expressing doubt, you can involve your team in a structured and focused problem-solving session: this is inclusive, action-focused and will lead to the decision and clarity that your team craves.

Ability to handle crises

Crises are your opportunity to shine. Managing is easy when things are going well. The test of a manager does not come in easy street: it comes when things go wrong. Do not avoid crises: embrace them as an opportunity.

Deal with any crisis in two ways. First, be decisive. Do not go into denial: deal with the problem fast and early. Unlike wine, crises rarely improve with age. They tend to get worse, especially when the politics of the blame game start up. Step up, while your peers step back. Quietly, everyone will be relieved that someone has the courage to take responsibility. To start with, any decision can be better than no decision. Curiously, the worse things are, the clearer things become. In the worst crises, there may be only one way out or one thing you can do. So do it. What matters is that you drive to action, create momentum, build hope and give a sense of clarity and purpose. Even if you then have to alter course, at least you have built momentum and you are going forwards.

The second part of dealing with the crisis is about how you are. Long after everyone has forgotten the details of who did what, they will remember how you behaved. This is where you have a choice. Some people will become invisible: they will stay out of the fray. Others will go into Machiavelli mode: they will do plenty of so-called helpful analysis, which happens to pin the blame on others, looks backwards and achieves nothing. Others may panic. A few will remain calm, positive, supportive and action-focused. If you look calm and in control, your team will have confidence in you. If you start an inquest into what went wrong, you will create the ideal breeding ground for infighting and politics.

How you behave is as important as what you do. Decide how you want to be seen, and then behave accordingly.

Honesty and integrity

Honesty and integrity have nothing to do with ethics. They are much more important than that: they are about survival and success. Without honesty and integrity, there can be no trust, and no teamwork. This sort of honesty is not a politician's honesty, which seems to mean: 'I am honest until I am found guilty of lying in a court of law.' Management honesty is much stronger: it means total discretion and having the strength to deal with uncomfortable situations early. If a team member is underperforming, it is dishonest and is a breach of trust not to deal with it until assessment time, when it becomes a surprise. Team members need to know where they stand, especially when they are in the wrong place.

Ultimately, honesty is about trust. No one wants to work with a boss they do not trust.

Honesty in investment banking

Investment banking is widely regarded as a shark pool. The leaders of investment banks should, therefore, be the biggest and meanest sharks in the pool. To discover whether this was true, I decided to interview some sharks.

Chris talked about the chairman of the investment bank:

'His defining characteristic is honesty. He never has a bad word to say about anyone. If you have a private conversation with him, you know it will stay private. He will not bad-mouth anyone behind their backs. If you waste his time or you are an idiot, the only negative consequence is that you will not get another meeting with him.

'Because of his honesty, everyone trusts him. Staff trust him. Clients trust him. This makes him very powerful in the market. Clients need people they can trust on very sensitive matters. Within the bank, he has virtually no enemies. His position is unassailable.'

Honesty is divisive. Leaders who rate poorly on honesty tend to rate poorly on everything else. Teams will not rate someone highly if they do not trust them. Leaders who are rated well on trust are not guaranteed good ratings elsewhere, but at least they get a chance to be rated fairly.

Being honest requires courage to have difficult conversations and make difficult decisions. In the short term, these may be awkward. In the long term, they are vital to acquiring the currency of leadership: trust and respect.

Chapter 4

Political management skills:

acquiring power to make things happen

In most organisations, you can find smart people and you can find nice people. You can even find people who are both smart and nice. But they are not necessarily the best or most successful managers. There are plenty of smart, nice people with high intelligence quotient (IQ) and high emotional quotient (EQ) who are eking out a quiet existence in the backwaters of the organisation. They are much liked but little used. Meanwhile, people who are not as smart or not as nice seem to levitate magically upwards through the organisation to positions of ever greater power.

The missing element for the smart, nice people is political quotient (PQ) skills: political intelligence.

Political skills sound very Machiavellian. At times, they can be Machiavellian. So it is worth being clear what political skills are about and what they are not about for the practising manager.

Political skills are the skills you need to make things happen in an organisation. IQ skills are intellectual, EQ skills are interpersonal and PQ skills are about the organisation and action. To make things happen, managers need to know how to acquire and use power and resources. Once some power has been acquired, it has to be used well to acquire more power and more resources. Often, this involves using power and resources over which the manager has no direct control.

In the last twenty years there have been two revolutions in management. The obvious one is about technology, which finally has come into the office and into the way managers work. In theory, office technology improves productivity. In practice, it does not. It fails for three reasons. First, it raises expectations rather than reduces workload. Because technology means we can be contacted at any time and anywhere, we are expected to respond any time and anywhere. Similarly, because it is now easier to produce presentations, presentations become longer but rarely better; we can copy people on email easily, so we do and we create more work without always having greater impact. Technology raises expectations but does not always raise performance.

Second, technology invites managers to do the wrong job. Because we can produce PowerPoint presentations ourselves, we do. And that is a complete waste of our time and effort, when there are other people who can do it better, faster and cheaper. If the best way we can add value is by producing our own PowerPoint presentations, we are probably in the wrong job.

Third, technology is a time waster. The amount of time wasted in offices on social media and other non-work technology is up to three hours a day, if some sources are to be believed. In any event, we have all, at times, been distracted from the task in hand by the wonders of the web.

So technology is clearly changing how we work. It should make managers more productive. More often it raises expectations, increases workloads, tempts us to do the wrong job and distracts us. We have to learn to master technology before it masters us.

The real revolution has been the way the job of the manager has changed. In the old world of command and control, managers made things happen through people they controlled. Now managers do not control all the resources they need to succeed. The job of a manager is to make things happen through people they do not control, and may not even like. That changes everything. You cannot order customers, colleagues, peers and bosses to do what you say. You have to learn a whole new set of skills: influencing, persuading, building a network of trust and support, making change happen, taking control without power and managing powerful people. This is the reality managers increasingly face, and these are the skills that are at the heart of PQ.

These skills – discussed in the following sections – are not mysterious. They are readily learnable skills that most managers can acquire to help both themselves and their organisations. PQ is about power. Like the Force in *Star Wars*, power can be put to good use or bad use. Each manager makes his or her own decision about becoming a wannabe Jedi Knight or a wannabe Darth Vader. Understanding the nature of power at least gives the manager the

> Understanding the nature of power at least gives the manager the choice.

choice. Failure to build PQ condemns managers to becoming a welcome doormat for more politically astute managers.

We will look at each of these skills in turn but, before we turn to the skills, it is worth looking at what political skills do not cover:

- Knifing your colleagues. There are ways of doing this: it can work in the short term but, in the long term, it results in many enemies and very little trust. That is a tough way to build a career.

- Bluffing your way to success. Perception management is important, but there has to be some substance behind the perception.

- Plotting the overthrow of your boss. If you try this, do not fail. The one unforgivable sin for a subordinate is disloyalty, and the boss has more power than you do. If you fail, you are finished.

In this chapter we will look first at a summary of the ten laws of power, and then explore in more detail those laws that you can use to best effect in your career.

4.1 The ten laws of power: achieving PQ

In the new world of PQ, power does not come just with your title. Even managers with big titles often struggle to gain control. Instead of formal power, effective managers learn to build informal power. They build and acquire influence, which goes far beyond their formal title: look around your own place of work and you will see people who do this well. They do not rely on some mysterious, genetic X-factor to do this. They all follow at least some of the simple rules.

These rules are tacit knowledge, not explicit. They are a set of know-how skills rather than know-what skills. These know-how skills become more important the more uncertain, ambiguous and challenging the situation becomes. These know-how skills are automatic reactions for the high PQ manager. They are like default settings in their mindset. Once you understand these automatic responses, you can start to learn them yourself. They can be described as the ten laws of power.

Here they are in summary:

1 Take control

Do not wait until you are CEO: high political quotient managers take some control at any level. Have a clear agenda and act on it. Your agenda can be told as a story in three parts:

1   This is where we are.
2   This is where we are going.
3   This is how we will get there.

By taking control, you create clarity, focus and purpose for yourself and colleagues. Even if they disagree, discussion will be focused on your agenda, not theirs. Taking control is especially important in crises and conflicts. Many people will hide: the high PQ manager will see an opportunity to make a mark.

2 Create loyal followers

You need to become the manager people want to follow, rather than have to follow. Then you will be able to attract the best teams and deliver the best results. But you also need loyal supporters beyond your own team. You will rely on colleagues and contractors to help you deliver results. Building support means building trust: you need to develop mutual understanding (shared values) and mutual respect – delivering on commitments. It is different from building friendships – trust is the core of professional relationships; friendship is the core of personal relationships.

3 Act the part

If you want to act and look like a junior manager, your wish will be granted – you will stay a junior manager. Observe how people two levels above you dress, talk and behave. If there is a gap between their behaviour and yours, think about changing.

Acting the part can be as shallow as dressing the way they dress – you should not be judged on how you dress, but you will be. But it is also more subtle. At senior levels, executives do not persuade each other with 300-page PowerPoint presentations. They talk through issues clearly.

Act as a partner to senior executives, not as their servant, and they are likely to treat you as more of an equal.

4 Strike early

Wherever there is uncertainty, high PQ managers use it to take control. You should be ready to step up, not back, when a crisis or opportunity emerges. Acting early takes courage.

Where it helps:

- Negotiating budgets. Agree broad objectives early, before the framework is dictated to you.
- Managing crises. If you have a plan for sorting out a crisis, you retain control. Acting late means it gets worse.
- Getting the right assignment. Waiting for a position to be advertised is too late. Your network should alert you to opportunities. Make sure you have positioned yourself with the right line managers to be placed where you want.

- Managing meetings and overcoming resistance. Never use a meeting to make a decision. By the time your agenda item goes to a meeting, you should know the decision will be positive. You should pre-empt all potential opposition in private meetings before the formal decision-making process.

5 Pick your battles

As long as there are insufficient resources to go around, there will be organisational conflict. High PQ managers will fight, but only where necessary.

Only fight:

- when there is a prize worth fighting for
- when you know you will win
- when there is no other way of achieving your goal.

Most corporate battles fail at least one, and sometimes all three, of these rules.

6 Be selectively unreasonable

When you accept excuses, you accept failure. High PQ managers know when to stretch people to achieve things they thought impossible. If you stretch people, they learn and develop, and so does the organisation.

> When you accept excuses, you accept failure.

Some managers take this to the extreme: they are always unreasonable and they do not stretch people as much as break them. Macho management trades off short-term gains for long-term destruction of human and economic capital. High PQ managers know how to build long-term performance by being unreasonable, selectively.

7 Build trust

Trust is the currency of power. If no one trusts you, do not expect to have much influence with anyone. Trust comes from doing as you say and always delivering on your commitments. This sounds easy, but it is not. What we say and what others hear are often quite different. When we talk, we think we are giving ourselves let-out clauses by saying, 'I hope to... I will try... I will look into it...'. We hope that excuses us when things do not work out: we will have hoped, tried and explored, even if the end outcome did not happen. What the other person heard was a promise: 'I will...'. Then you can argue you did as you said, but arguing semantics does not restore trust. It is far better to have a difficult conversation early rather than late. Be brutal about setting expectations and reinforcing them so that there can be no surprises at the end.

8 Embrace ambiguity

Where there is ambiguity, there is often a vacuum waiting to be filled by a high PQ manager. It arises out of uncertain agendas, such as:

- How shall we organise the offsite team meeting?
- Who should work on this new project?
- How shall we respond to this new competitive move?

Move in early and take control of selected opportunities. The high PQ manager stands out as someone positive and action-focused. They need to deliver successfully to gain any credit.

Then the very high PQ manager conspicuously shares credit with everyone else, ensuring support from others while reinforcing the fact they were in control.

9 Focus on outcomes

This should be obvious, but many managers find it safer to focus on analysis, processes and problems. Outcome focus minimises unnecessary conflicts: instead of playing the blame game, it is forward looking and drives action. Outcome focus starts with asking the right questions:

- Meetings – what do I want to achieve, regardless of the formal agenda?

- Conflict with another department – what do I want to achieve and is it worth fighting for?

- Crises and setbacks – what outcomes do we need, not who is to blame?

10 Use it or lose it

Once you get your hands on the levers of power, use them. The better you do so, the more formal power you will acquire. Use them poorly, and you will lose them and, possibly, your job.

Avoid the trap of playing safe: it is legitimate if your only goal is survival. If you want to succeed, you have to make a difference.

Ask yourself: 'What will be different as a result of my performance in this role?' What will your legacy be? Use power to make a real difference.

The ten laws of influence

1 Take control

Have a clear plan for your department; know what will be different as a result of your work; build the right team and get the right budget and support for your plan. Do not accept as sacrosanct the plan, team and budget that you inherit.

2 Create loyal followers

Show you are genuinely interested in each member of your team and their careers; understand their needs; manage their expectations; build trust by having difficult conversations positively and early; always deliver on your commitments to them.

3 **Act the part**

Act like other influential people in your organisation; be positive, confident and assertive; act like a peer to senior staff, not like their bag carrier.

4 **Strike early**

Latecomers to assignments, discussions and new initiatives struggle to shape the outcome. The earlier you strike, the more you influence what happens. This is riskier than sitting back and waiting to join the bandwagon. But, if you want to influence, lead the bandwagon, do not join it later.

5 **Pick your battles**

Only fight when there is a prize worth fighting for; only fight when you know you will win; only fight when there is no other way of achieving your goal. It is better to win a friend than it is to win an argument.

6 **Be selectively unreasonable**

Dare to stretch yourself, your team and others: make a difference by going beyond business as usual and beyond the comfort zone – this lets you learn, make an impact and build influence.

7 **Build trust**

Trust is the currency of power. Without trust, no one will trust you. Do what you say and always deliver on commitments. Building trust leads to influence; building popularity leads to weakness, which comes from always compromising and conceding to please other people.

8 **Embrace ambiguity**

Crises and uncertainty are wonderful opportunities to make a mark, take control and fill the void of uncertainty and doubt that others create. Ambiguity lets leaders flourish.

9 **Focus on outcomes**

Work to clear goals that have visibility and impact across the organisation. Drive to action, not analysis.

10 **Use it or lose it**

Control your destiny or someone else will; you remain influential only if you use your influence.

4.2 Taking control: the power of ideas

In the old world, power and control came from formal sources of authority. These included:

- Control of budgets: a manager's empire was defined by the size of their budget. The bigger the budget, the better. This led to highly dysfunctional empire building that did nothing to control costs and increase efficiency.

- Control of information.

- Control of staff and skills. If you and your team have a unique set of skills on which the firm depends, you have power. Until you are outsourced.

- Control of customers. If cash is king, then your customer is the queen and wields the real power. In professional service firms, power goes to the rain makers who help customers part with their cash.

- Control of permissions. This is the world of the jobsworth ('It's more than my job's worth to let you do that...'). Petty officials who have little control do not cede it easily: it is their only source of power and purpose.

All of these sources of power still have some relevance today. They are bargaining chips that you can play with. Put simply, if you have no budget, information, staff, skills, customers or permissive authority, you will not have much influence with anyone anywhere.

But these sources of power are not enough: they are simply your entry ticket into the world of influence. If the first challenge is to acquire some of these sources of power, the second and greater challenge is to know how to put them to use.

In the new world of management, just because you have the title and formal authority, it does not mean you are in control. Taking control can be difficult, even for the most senior managers. If you are following an agenda that you inherited with a team and a budget from your predecessor, you are not in control. You are simply administering a legacy. Worse, you will be at the mercy of the competing agendas and priorities of all your peers and colleagues in other departments. So, how do you take control?

Having a very clear, relevant and worthwhile agenda is at the heart of control in a world of ambiguity. Your agenda should be an idea about how your department or unit will be different and better as a result of your leadership. You have to describe a future perfect that your team can work towards and that top management will support. This will help you cut through the day-to-day noise of management and let you focus on what is important, not just on what is urgent.

There is a huge amount of noise for you to deal with. There are daily mini crises and conflicts. There is an endless stream of reporting and administration. Annual budgets and performance reviews are events to which all managers must apply themselves. But they are simply a means to an end: the objective of management is not to deliver budget papers and performance reviews. Managers have to achieve budgets and performance. This normally means that you have to do something different from what was happening before. Doing the same as before and expecting a better result than before is an exercise in wishful thinking. If all you do is deal with the noise, you will not make a difference.

Sometimes this is called having a vision. This conjures up images of Martin Luther King and 'I have a dream...' Most managers,

> A vision is no more than a simple story.

who have a vision like that, should keep it to themselves. In management terms, a vision is no more than a simple story that has three parts:

1   This is where we are going.
2   This is how we are going to get there.
3   This is how you can help.

Some people add an optional fourth statement: 'This is where we are.' This simply helps explain the relevance and importance of where we are going. Dwelling too long on the present and the past is not a good way of driving to the future.

1 This is where we are going

Giving direction is one of the keys to management. Direction needs to be consistent and predictable. The team needs to have some way of understanding your priorities and making choices without always referring back to you. They need to know where to focus their personal efforts. This is where it helps to have a simple story that tells your team where they should be trying to get to.

Typically, where we are going will be either a clear goal, or a relevant theme. Goals might include:

- Make budget this year.
- Acquire three new clients this year.
- Cut costs by 15 per cent.
- Introduce one new product.
- Create a new test market programme.

Themes could include ideas like:

- Professionalise the way we work.
- Accelerate decision making.
- Become more customer-focused.
- Simplify work processes and patterns.

The Soviet pin factory

The Five Year Plan had been approved with its usual 100 per cent support. Gosplan now had to convert the plan into detail. Eventually, it got round to the target for pins. The Plan called for a 500 per cent increase in the quantity of pins produced. Seeing the sense of economies of scale, Gosplan decided to focus one factory on producing 'Pins for the People'.

The factory, which had been turning out Glorious and Revolutionary tractors, was dismayed to see that it was required to produce 20 tonnes of pins a year. The staff were all tractor heads, and did not fancy becoming pin heads. The factory manager devised a plan to meet the goal in one week, leaving the other 51 weeks for the business of tractor making.

At the end of week one, the factory had produced one giant 20-tonne pin, which would be of no use to even the stoutest babushka.

At the end of week two, the factory manager was helping fulfil the Soviet salt-mining goal and Gosplan was wondering if there might be more to this business of setting targets...

Some managers combine a goal and a theme: the theme is the method by which they will achieve the goal. Making things this simple takes effort, insight and judgement. Once a manager has a story like this, the path to control is clear: the manager has crafted an agenda with which to drive the team and focus it. The manager controls events, rather than being controlled by events.

2 This is how we are going to get there

Saying where you want to go is the easy bit: getting there is harder. Once you have a destination in mind, you will need to show that the goal is:

● relevant to the needs of the department

● achievable.

Most important is to focus on a few easy wins. Everyone likes to feel that they are backing a winner. A one-year goal for the department is too big: find some things that the team can start working on now so it can start seeing some early progress. You do not need to lay out the whole year in advance, as long as you are clear about the end point and the starting point.

3 This is how you can help

This is where you have to convert a general story about the department into a story that is relevant to each team member. People like to feel wanted, so show that they are important and can contribute.

Review the departmental goals individually with each team member. This is a great opportunity to set expectations about what you want to achieve and how you want to work. In return, expect to hear what team members want from you in terms of their careers, opportunities, skills and working style. As with the team as a whole, identify for each team member some early wins where they can start to make a contribution and make progress. This builds confidence on both sides: if they are unable to deliver some agreed, simple and early wins, it may be time to get worried about performance and capability.

Do this well and you will have created a psychological contract with each team member where you are both committed to what each other wants. You will have taken control of both the team as a whole and each individual within it through mutually agreed goals, actions and working styles.

4.3 Managing change: people, not projects

The received wisdom is that management is all about change. Perhaps it should be. But most managers most of the time are not keen on change. It represents risk, uncertainty and even more effort than the regular day job. The only people who are addicted to change are management consultants (change means fees and they are not at risk from the consequences of their actions) and CEOs (change tells

> The only people who are addicted to change are management consultants and CEOs.

the board that they are doing something and, since they are in control of the change, they have little to fear from it).

Because change is seen to be central to management, management naturally claims to be implementing change. There are retail financial institutions and public sector institutions where they do little more than change the wall calendar once a year, but even they will talk about the ever-increasing pace of change and the challenge it represents. This perception may be wholly false. Perceptions may be imaginary, but the consequences of them are real. If managers feel that they are already changing fast, then any more change will take them well outside their comfort zone. Suddenly, you will hear many clever and rational arguments about why the change is very risky and doomed to cause chaos. Rational arguments are often no more than a plea for help from threatened individuals.

Change is the land of FUD: fear, uncertainty and doubt. Managers do not like to go there.

Change, like people, is not easy to put in neat little boxes. In principle, people should not be put in boxes until they are dead. But behind this messy reality, there are some consistent rules of success and failure. Every film is unique, but most follow familiar themes. The same is true of change: each change is unique and succeeds or fails in its own unique way. But there are common themes behind both the successes and failures. Learning from personal experience is painful: what follows will help you learn from the experience of others.

We will explore the two main aspects of successful change:

- setting up change to succeed
- managing the change process.

Setting up change to succeed

Most change efforts succeed or fail before they even start. As a manager, you have to invest time before you start to set up your team for success. Over the years, there has been one way of predicting which change efforts will succeed or fail and it can be summarised in an equation. Here it is in all its spurious mathematical accuracy:

$$N \times V \times C \geqslant R$$

where:

> N is the need for change
>
> V is the vision of what the change will achieve
>
> C is the capacity to change
>
> R are the risks and costs of change

What the change equation says, in plain English, is that you need a strong perceived need for change, a vision of what you will achieve and you must have the capacity to change. All of that must exceed the risks and costs of your change effort.

Let us explore what each element means in practice, and how you can put it to use.

Need for change

Given that most people do not instinctively like change, you need to find a real reason for change. You have to have a problem you are solving. Put human nature to use: if people are risk averse, then they are change averse.

You can overcome risk aversion by showing that the risk of doing nothing is greater than the risk of doing something. Even CEOs will use this tactic. They will create a 'burning platform' that makes change essential to survival. The essence of the burning platform story is that competition, regulators or technology is about to put us out of business unless we change. Faced with the prospect of losing your job or changing the way you work, most people will elect to change the way they work.

As a manager, you have to show that you are addressing a real problem. Ideally, this is not a problem you have created. It can be a challenge that your firm as a whole faces. Listen to what the CEO and top management is talking about. They will talk about the challenges they face. Many managers half listen to such speeches and then do nothing: they wait to see if they need to do anything. But this is your chance to shine: show that you have not just listened but you are also acting on top management priorities.

Delighting the customer

The CEO made his state of the nation speech. It was the usual attempt to inspire both hope and fear: hope of a better future and fear of the consequences if there was no change. He also banged on about delighting the customer, which was not a big surprise since this was a law firm that depended on delighting customers. Most people nodded and then went on to lunch.

The facilities manager had not been invited to the meeting: he was far too unimportant. But he was there anyway, making sure that the seating, sound, video and lunch were all working.

He thought about the speech. What on earth had delighting customers got to do with facilities? He was not sure, so he called his team together.

The first thing they did was to sort out the toilets: it is hard to delight customers with second-rate toilets. They became a feature in their own right. Then they changed reception to make it more inviting. Receptionists had slowly morphed into becoming security, so he changed that by empowering the receptionists to become concierges: do what it takes to help visitors. And they created a client suite of meeting rooms, which were not just pleasant, they were also secure.

At the next annual meeting, the CEO did not ignore the facilities manager. He asked the facilities manager to address all the partners: he was the one person who had really understood the CEO's message about delighting the customer and had acted on it.

Understand top management's agenda and act on it: that way you will find powerful support and you will build your presence and credibility.

Vision of change

A vision is simply a grand way of talking about your idea, which we looked at in the previous section. Show how the change will make things different and better, not just for your unit, but for each team member in it, and for the organisation as a whole.

The need for change creates pressure; your vision of change creates hope, direction and focus. You need both pressure and hope. If you have pressure but no hope, then you get despair because no one knows how to respond. Once you set out your vision, it becomes clearer to each team member what they should do.

A good vision will have clear, definable and time-limited benefits. Each team member should know what success looks like, and when they should get there. Top management should also see benefits from the change. Broadly, benefits fall into three categories: qualitative, quantitative (non-financial) and financial. Your team is probably least interested in driving financial benefits; top management are most interested in financial benefits. The greater the benefits they see, the more likely they are to support you. That means you have to find ways of articulating the prize to each group, as in the table below.

> A good vision will have clear, definable and time-limited benefits.

Sizing the prize of your vision

Qualitative benefits	Quantitative benefits	Financial benefits
Increase customer focus	Improve customer retention from 80% to 90% annually	Increase annual revenues by £2.5 million
Raise team morale	Reduce voluntary staff turnover from 18% to 10%	Save £300,000 on recruiting and training costs

In the simplified cases above, you need all three ways of sizing the prize. The qualitative idea is what everyone will understand; the quantitative benefits give tangible goals for your team to work towards; the financial benefits are the prize that top management will back.

You need to keep on coming back to your prize. You will, inevitably, face passive and active opposition. If all you talk about is increasing customer focus, it is hard to deal with such resistance. But, if you can dangle a £2.5 million prize in front of people, it becomes much harder to resist. No one wants to be the manager who stopped the firm making £2.5 million a year.

Capacity to change

Ultimately, this is about having the right support to make change happen. As ever, the devil is in the detail of what this means in practice.

The right support comes in three flavours. You need:

- A powerful sponsor. Your idea or vision should be directly supporting this top manager: they need to see that they will benefit from what you are doing. They will then help you secure the right budget, secure the right team and help you unblock any political obstacles you face on the way. They will not be involved day to day: if they are the right sponsor they will be too busy. But they offer you critical support to get change started and to keep change going.

- Technical support. If you want to claim that your change effort will increase revenues by £2.5 million annually, then that is a claim that has to be validated to be credible. Sales and marketing need to validate that customer retention can be improved; finance need to confirm that your financial projections are correct.

- The right team. This is only partly about skills. More important is mindset and values. To make change work you need team members with initiative, drive, resilience and creativity to deal with setbacks. They also need good people skills. A good test of your sponsor is whether they can help you get the right team. If you land up with the B team, walk away: it is a recipe for sleepless nights and under-delivery, and is a sign that either your sponsor lacks power or it is not a high priority for them.

Risks and costs of change

All change is costly and risky, which is why most people do not like it. The costs and risks that are easy to deal with are the rational costs and risks. This is the land of the risk log and issue log, with all its mitigating actions. These rational risks normally can be managed rationally. The killer risks are not rational: they are emotional and political:

● Emotional risks are deeply personal: how will this change affect me? Will I still have a job? Will I have new targets, a new boss or a new role? Will I have to learn new skills? Who will gain the credit for success and will I get all the blame if it goes wrong?

● Political risks are about power and position: how will this affect my unit? Will I gain or lose budget, staff and responsibilities? How will this affect my unit's agenda and priorities?

Naturally, no one talks directly about these risks because they do not appear professional. Instead, anyone who feels threatened will start raising a whole raft of apparently rational objections to your change idea. Arguing the rational case becomes an exercise in futility. No matter whether you think you are right or wrong, the other side simply will dig in deeper. Once they take a position in public, they will find it very hard to change their position.

Your best solution is to talk to key people and influencers in private. Make sure you understand and respect their needs; give them a sense of involvement in what you are doing so that they feel less threatened. Use the influencing and persuading techniques outlined elsewhere in the book.

As you start your change effort, keep the change equation in mind. There is no point in investing a large amount of time and effort in a change, unless you have set it up for success. The setup may take time, but it is time well spent because it will save you far more time and grief later on if you do it right from the start.

Managing the change process

The change process is much more than project management, which we will deal with later. Project management is vital: it deals with what has to happen when. Change management is about people and politics. Good change managers and good project managers are often very different species: one is good with people, the other is good with tasks.

First, we will look at the nature of the change process and how you can deal with it, and then we will look at the specific problem of dealing with resistance to change.

The nature of the change journey

Change rarely runs smoothly. It can be a roller coaster (as illustrated in the Change and the valley of death figure on page 205). Each person has a different journey through this roller coaster, so you need to help each person individually.

There are some practical ways of helping people through this emotional roller coaster. If they become too stressed, they will become dysfunctional. They need your help to stay productive. The key principles are:

- **Incremental commitments**. Do not ask people to do too much too soon. Stage their commitments. Start with something easy for them to do. This has two effects:

    1　It builds their confidence: they perceive that they can succeed.

    2　It creates a sense of obligation: having started, they will feel obliged to see the whole effort through.

- **Stretch, but do not break people**. Change, if it is serious, will take people outside their comfort zones. This can be exciting for them and lead to increased performance, if they are well managed. But, if they are stretched too far, they become too stressed. Like a mountaineer getting altitude sickness, they need to go all the way back to their comfort zone to recover. Then the process of staged commitments, increasing commitment and stretch can start slowly again. A common mistake is to keep forcing the pace instead of giving people proper recovery time. Look after the people, and they will look after the tasks. Do not let the tasks defeat the people.

- **Focus on the positives**. Recognise and reinforce the right behaviours and performance. Find something that each person is doing well, recognise it and build their confidence. Where there are problems, help the team drive to solutions and action as fast as possible: do not let them dwell on problems and on what they cannot do. Even if there is only a small thing they can do to contribute to a big problem, get them to do it.

- **Be firm on goals, flexible on the means**. Goal focus is not just about what must be achieved, but why it must be achieved. Achieving the goal will have positive consequences for the organisation and the individual: keep them focused on that prize so they see the value and relevance of what they are doing. But then allow them flexibility over how they get there: give them a sense of empowerment, control and responsibility.

- **Set expectations early**. If people expect to go through a valley of death, they do not panic when things get tough. We told one CEO to expect a valley of death experience. For the next two months he was like a child asking, 'Are we there, yet?' at each new setback. He steered the organisation calmly through the tough period because he was ready for it.

- **Find some early wins**. A few symbolic acts often will help convince people that you are serious about this change and that there is real momentum. People will start to climb aboard the bandwagon when they see it is moving.

This different journeys that can be experienced through this roller coaster are illustrated in the following figure.

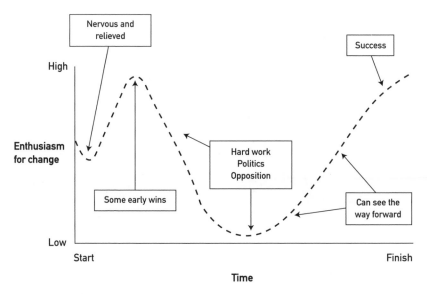

Change and the valley of death

Dealing with resistance to change

Most of the principles of managing resistance are covered in more detail under sections 3.2: Persuading people: how to sell anything and 3.5: Handling conflict: from FEAR to EAR. If the project has been set up the right way, most of the resistance will have been overcome before the project even starts.

But one danger lurks. Any change attracts resistance. The resistance will be most vocal from people who perceive that they have the most to lose (see the figure overleaf). They will make a large amount of noise. Meanwhile, the majority will keep silent. You can see the same effect when the Government changes tax and spending priorities. The losers make a huge fuss; the winners keep very quiet.

The trap for the PQ manager is getting bogged down in debate with the minority. The more you listen to those in the minority, the more you legitimise their point of view. In effect, you give them a veto over your programme. At worst they will stop it; at best they will merely delay it, weaken it and cause huge disruption.

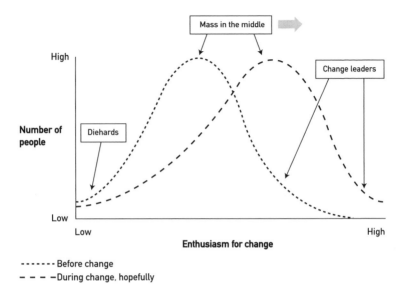

Shifting the change bell curve

The best way to deal with such obstacles is to navigate around them. Focus your efforts on enthusing the mass of people (and the critical opinion formers and decision makers). As they begin to give their tacit support to your efforts, the resistance army will start to feel isolated. As the train leaves the station, they will have a choice: get on the train, stay behind or lie on the tracks in front of the train. No matter what: the train will not stop. In business, the resistance army will break down slowly: some will join you, some will go into hiding and some may seek other opportunities elsewhere.

4.4 People and change: through the valley of death

Project managers often like to call themselves change managers, because it sounds much more sophisticated. They are following the same road as personnel (whoops: human capital management, strategic talent management) and sales (whoops again: client relationship officers, key account managers, market executives, development associates).

Behind the harmless semantics, there is some serious confusion. Project management is largely an IQ skill that focuses on building or, sometimes, changing things like IT systems, production lines and major civil engineering works. Typically, it will involve the following sorts of activities:

- drawing up job specifications
- creating risk and issue logs
- sizing the job – people, time, materials, money
- defining the critical path and what tasks need to happen in which order – put the foundations in before building the roof; open the door before trying to walk through it
- measuring and monitoring progress
- creating project plans with all the symbols that show decision points and pathways that most of us struggle to understand.

These are highly valuable disciplines that are essential when managing complex tasks.

At the end of a well-managed project, things will have changed. But people will not have changed simply as a result of building a new factory or IT system. To make a project truly succeed, you have to change what people do and how they do things as well. This is the essence of change management as opposed to project management. It returns us to the heart of the role of a manager: making things happen through other people.

Effective change management is about people, not just projects. We will explore five of the most common ways to affect people in the organisation:

> Effective change management is about people, not just projects.

1 Changing what they do: roles, responsibilities, job descriptions.

2 Changing how they do things: skills.

3 Changing how they and their tasks are organised: processes and procedures.

4   Changing how they are measured, rewarded and recognised: information, measurement, appraisal and incentive systems.

5   Changing how people behave: cultural change in its widest sense.

The high IQ skills of project management do not help a manager faced with the deep EQ and PQ requirements of change management: changing people. Unlike buildings or IT systems, people have minds of their own with their own hopes and fears. They will argue back, avoid and evade, cause trouble, act emotionally and politically. They will act in their own self-interest, tempered by the interests of the organisation. Change is a messy reality that does not lend itself to being captured on neat little critical path analyses with elegant box and wire diagrams in a piece of project management software.

1 Changing what people do

Reorganising often is taken to mean structural change: moving the boxes around the organisation chart in the hope that something better will happen as a result. Structural change meets with increasing cynicism from managers who have seen it all before: centralisation to decentralisation and back again, organising around products, customers, functions or markets, according to the fashion *du jour*.

There are three sides to any reorganisation: IQ, EQ and PQ. The intellectual, rational reason for the reorganisation is the most common and least effective reason for the reorganisation. The benefits of reorganisation come from its emotional and political impact, if this is well handled:

● **Rational aspects of reorganising**. This is where consultants get very excited and draw up lots of charts, do job sizing and profiling and create countless job descriptions. Often they create needless complexity and bureaucracy to justify themselves. The real problem with the rational approach to reorganisation is that very often there is no way of knowing, or proving, that one organisation structure is definitively better than another.

- **Emotional aspects of reorganising**. Reorganising at its most basic level is a call to arms for the organisation. It is a way of saying something like: 'We have to get closer to the customer, so now we are moving away from a product-focused structure to a customer-focused structure.' Change the structure and back that up with changes in measures, rewards, processes and procedures, and people will start to believe the story. At an individual level, the reorganisation is a great opportunity to reset the psychological contract with each member of the team: it is a way of saying, 'Here is a new world, now let's work out what we both have to do to succeed in that new world.' (See the boxed example overleaf.)

- **Political aspects of reorganising**. A very good reason to reorganise is to overthrow the power barons. For example, Martha was appointed to run the European operations of a large systems house. In a highly macho culture, the power barons were determined to keep her at bay. They all had elegant reasons why their part of the organisation was unique and could not help the cost drive. So Martha reorganised the entire team (with one ritual execution of a power baron who was offered an unacceptable job and left). She moved the firm from a geographic focus to an industry focus (financial services, oil and gas, public sector, etc.). The rational argument was the need to build greater industry expertise. The real reason was to break the power of the power barons. They found themselves in unfamiliar territory; they could not use their old excuses and they had seen what resistance led to. Martha was now very firmly in control of the macho barons.

Setting the new psychological contract

It was a Sunday morning. We knew we had to announce the reorganisation tomorrow morning. Everything was in place: the piles of job descriptions, the PowerPoint presentations, the Q&A sheet, the organisation charts and the web pages. And it felt hollow: there was something missing. We looked at all the paper and realised that what was missing were the people: they had been lost in the deluge of analysis.

We started to think about each individual and what it meant for them personally: their hopes and fears and what we needed from them to make the reorganisation become a success. Slowly, the reorganisation came to life.

For each individual we identified:

- what would be different for them
- how the reorganisation could help them personally
- their likely personal concerns and how we could help them
- what we needed from them in terms of changed performance, skills or style.

As the reorganisation rolled out, we sat down with each individual and discussed this new psychological contract: our commitments to each other. This psychological contract between each boss and his or her team members turned out to be far more powerful than the dry job descriptions that rapidly got consigned to the waste-paper basket.

2 Changing how people do things

Raising and changing skills is a constant struggle for managers themselves and for the people they manage.

The manager's career journey is marked by a complete change in the sorts of skills he or she needs to master. Early in a career, managers need to learn their trade. These craft skills may be accounting, IT, law or marketing. For the most part, people are keen to learn such skills:

- They know they do not yet have mastery of their craft.
- They know that mastery is essential to career progression.
- The knowledge is well documented and can be learned with effort.

These craft skills become decreasingly important as the manager's career progresses. Someone who is still cutting code or doing stock checks for the audit is, probably, not a senior manager.

The skills that become far more important are people skills: getting other people to do things. A manager who cannot get other people to do things is not managing.

> A manager who cannot get other people to do things is not managing.

Simple observation within your own organisation will show a few managers who can do this very well, and many more who are somewhere between adequate and abysmal.

The toughest challenge is to learn and then upgrade people skills: motivating, influencing, delegating, directing and managing conflict and different styles. But this is where training fails badly. An extraordinary number of managers find that they are busy arranging yoga lessons for their cat, or whatever their excuse may be, which means that they cannot attend your lovingly crafted people skills workshop. People skills training has precisely the wrong dynamics compared to craft skills training:

- Most managers do not want to admit that they have poor people skills: going on a training course is seen as a sign of weakness. And most managers like to think they are good with people.
- Managers do not see the relevance of the workshops to their careers: they will have far more pressing needs to meet some immediate challenges.

- The skills required are not well understood or well documented: we are dealing with tacit knowledge, not explicit knowledge. Into this vacuum step both charlatans and gurus who claim to have found the answer: all their answers contradict each other and it is not clear that their solution fits your problem anyway. They offer one miracle solution for all problems from drooping morale to drooping profits.

Most of us trust experience not training. That makes sense. We see someone do something well, and we might try to copy it.

This gives managers the clues about how they can enhance the people skills of themselves and their teams. There are three basic mechanisms:

1 **Coaching**. This is covered in more detail in section 3.3: Coaching: no more training.

2 **Peer group learning**. Let people learn from each other about what really works (see the boxed example opposite). The essence of this is to create a structured journey of observation and discovery. Tap into the collective experience of the group and identify what works in practice in the current context. Done well, this is also an opportunity to help people rethink what they do. Learning from peers has credibility and relevance, which few outsiders can match, but it has to be well structured.

3 **Building hinterland fast**. Good managers tend to have hinterland. They have a range of experiences and perspectives to draw on when faced with unfamiliar challenges. This is where outsiders can help – not by offering answers, but by offering alternative perspectives and experiences. No single experience or perspective will work for everyone: the idea is to give enough alternatives to allow people to learn from what they want to. At the risk of shameless self-promotion, my work with indigenous tribes in Papua New Guinea and Mongolia, in the Arctic (the Saami) and with the Tuareg (Mali and Libya) gives managers an insight into ways of surviving environments that are even tougher than most business environments. (See www.leadershippartnership.com.)

Peer group learning in practice

Teaching experienced sales people to sell is dangerous. They think they know it all. And, when it comes to the arcane world of life insurance products, any trainer is right to feel fear. So we turned the confidence of the sales people on its head. We let them show off.

First, we analysed who was best at selling different products to different customers. We developed a very basic selling model with them (see section 3.2: Persuading people: how to sell anything). We then got the best sales people together in groups to share their secrets. This was their moment of glory. They all tried to outdo each other with their insight, which we duly documented.

We structured their output and rolled it out in workshops, which got everyone else to build on the frameworks and insights of the top sales people. Everyone else was very keen to take part in these events: understanding how the best sales people really worked was a recipe for increasing their own personal sales and annual bonuses.

At the end of the process, we had a sales formula that would fail certainly in theory: it succeeded wildly in practice.

3 Changing how people and tasks are organised

Process change is very powerful and very misused. Used well, it helps an organisation improve marketplace performance in terms of quality, cost and customer experience. The essence of process change is to turn the organisation on its side. Most organisations tend to think functionally. This is human nature. We all look at the world from where we stand, be it in customer service, logistics, operations or any of the support functions. This makes it difficult to achieve two things:

- **Cost efficiency.** We can cut departmental costs, but many of our costs are driven by the demands of other departments and we cannot see what knock-on effects our cost cuts will have elsewhere. Cost cutting in the absence of process focus is a crude hacking at costs that results in political turf battles as each department tries to protect its own territory. Recessions lead to cost hacking. Like a surgeon amputating a leg with gangrene, the patient may survive but will not be fitter as a result.

● **Market effectiveness.** The traditional functional view of the world encourages each department to see other departments as their customer. The real customer, who buys our services and pays our bills, becomes an invisible and remote being.

Cost inefficiency and market ineffectiveness are not a recipe for success. Good process focus overturns the functional focus. By looking at a process (new product development, order fulfilment, customer service, trade execution) from end to end, managers can see how their departmental actions link together. Managers rarely see how they fit into the whole business (from sheep to shop in the rag trade, or from soup to nuts for gastronomes). Once they can see the big picture, they can improve things by playing a managerial equivalent of a parlour game called 'Just a Minute'. In this game, you have to speak for a minute without repeating the same word, without hesitating and without deviating. It is fiendishly difficult to do this. The re-engineering equivalent of 'Just a Minute' is to redesign a core business process so that it works without:

● hesitation – avoids any delays in the process

● deviation – avoids any unnecessary activities that add no value

● repetition – avoids rework as a result of poor quality.

The result should be a process that achieves success in the corporate challenge of betterfastercheaper.

To succeed, process redesign needs to start with the customer. Start by working out what the customer experience should look like, and work back from there. Do not start with what you already have: it may be broken. Incremental improvement of a broken system simply helps the bad survive longer. Starting with a blank sheet of paper based on customer needs gives you a chance to focus the organisation successfully.

> Incremental improvement of a broken system simply helps the bad survive longer.

The downsides of process redesign are great. In many cases, re-engineering has become cost cutting with a smile, where the smile is an optional extra. It has become a dirty word. Mention re-engineering, and people imagine hordes of junior consultants arriving to map your existing processes in great detail and at great expense before firing you.

Delivering successful process redesign is a corporate overhaul that includes: rethinking how to serve the customer; redesigning processes; changing the structure, rewards, measure and information systems to support the new redesign; changing skill sets; changing the way people work. It is ambitious and requires very strong political support. Few managers get to initiate a true, company-wide process redesign. If you hear that such a redesign is going to happen, it normally pays to be on the inside helping the redesign. Being on the outside, your risk of being redesigned out of a job increases dramatically.

A short history of business processes

Around 1996 the West rediscovered the art of changing processes and called it process re-engineering. Japan had been focused on process re-engineering for a long time, except they called it things like *kaizen* and TQM. They scared the West out of deep complacency, which helped everyone except for the employees of industries they decimated.

The West itself had always known of the importance of processes, but somehow had forgotten about them. Adam Smith, in his book *The Wealth of Nations*, describes the extraordinary productivity and quality gains that could be achieved through process management in pin making. A single artisan pin maker executing the whole process was slow and inefficient. A group of unskilled workers, each of whom performed one small step in the pin-making process, could achieve extraordinary quality and productivity. In this one visit, Adam Smith got to the heart of successful capitalism and management practice: specialisation and the subdivision of labour.

From Adam Smith to Henry Ford it was a very small intellectual leap. Ford swept away the artisan car builders by installing and perfecting the production line. As with the pin makers of Gloucester, he discovered that low-skilled but well-organised workers could achieve quality and quantity beyond the reach of any artisan.

The power of process re-engineering was demonstrated by Dell. Michael Dell, as a young graduate, took on the might of IBM, Apple, Toshiba, HP and Compaq in the PC market. He had nothing going for him. Perhaps out of desperation, because he could not afford to have any stock, he decided to sell his computers to order and direct to the public. In one fell swoop he had re-engineered the entire industry as follows:

- Traditional PC process flow: make, then hope to sell.
- Dell PC process flow: sell, then hope to make.

This is re-engineering made simple, beyond the wire diagrams of process re-engineers. The effect of this one change was to:

- eliminate all finished stock
- make growth cash positive: customers pay you before you pay your suppliers
- eliminate losses from unsold stock, write-downs and fire sales
- eliminate the need for sophisticated sales forecasting tools
- reduce costs by eliminating expensive resellers
- gain very good and fast knowledge about customer and market trends
- beat the competition.

Good re-engineering has two characteristics, which Dell showed:

1 It is simple, not complicated.

2 It is focused on market pressures, not internal pressures.

Most process redesign fails these two tests.

4 Changing how people are measured, rewarded and recognised

Two of the oldest adages in management are still two of the truest: 'You can control only what you measure' and 'You get only what you reward'. Core to the manager's task is to measure and reward the right things. Here are some good ways not to do it:

● Measure call centre staff on number of calls handled: allow the customers to suffer from poor service as call centre staff rush to get through each call.

● Minimise warranty claims: watch managers erect huge barriers to claims from customers (must pre-register the product after sale, produce the original till receipt, stamped warranty document and original packaging, pay for the postage to Vladivostok, produce evidence that the fault is not subject to any of the 317 exemption clauses in the warranty document and then have the submission signed and approved by all eight of your great-grandparents).

● Measure bank calling officers on the volume of loans advanced: then discover that lending money is easy, but getting it back is difficult, if you have not paid proper attention to loan quality. This is a basic truth of banking, which earlier versions of this book warned of. It is a basic truth that seems to have eluded many highly paid bankers.

● Measure software writers on KLOCs (thousands of lines of code written): get huge amounts of complicated code, which is hard to change, instead of fewer, more elegant and more robust code. Measure book writers the same way and you would be in trouble.

The only simple answer to the question, 'How should I measure performance?' is 'Measure it well.' This is as simple as it is unhelpful. Sometimes, questions are more helpful than answers. Here are the key ones to ask:

- What is important to the organisation as a whole currently? This creates the context for setting and refocusing rewards and measures in your area. Make sure your goals align with the corporate drive for customer retention, cost reduction, or rapid growth of skills, staff and sales.

- What do I really need to measure? Be careful what you wish for. Remember King Midas in Greek mythology wished that all he touched would turn to gold. He cursed his wish when he found his food, wine, wife and mistresses turning to gold. In reality, you will need a mixture of financial, market, organisation and development measures (see the boxed example opposite).

- How will people react? Think through the consequences of human behaviour. People will take the shortest route to your goal, and shortcuts are not always good.

- How will I recognise and reward performance? Human nature is curious here. People tend to spend disproportionate emotional energy on what is visible and discretionary. This means that core salary does not drive performance. But bonuses, prizes, company cars, titles and perks receive huge amounts of attention. These are important because they are visible to colleagues and they feel like something we can control directly.

- What unintended consequences will this goal have? One way to find out is to ask yourself what games you would play if you were set the same goal. Work out what shortcuts, priority changes, pointless cost cuts or data manipulation you could use to hit the goal. Rest assured that all those games will be played by others, if not by you.

Putting in place effective measurement systems: from data to information

It was the trip in the elevator to the CEO that got me worried about the company measurement systems. At the third floor, a porter pushed a low loader into the elevator with about 30 kg of computer printout. I asked him what it was. 'This week's reports for Steve (the CEO),' he said cheerfully. Steve did not even like reading.

We both went to see Steve, who groaned at the gigabytes of rubbish that had just come through the door.

So we sat down and I asked him to draw up on one side of paper the measures he really wanted to see each week. The important stuff fitted easily on to one sheet of paper. We then started to trawl through the computer printout and found that what he really wanted was not in all the data he received. Inadvertently, we had discovered the balanced scorecard, but lacked the wit to copyright it. The information Steve required answered four basic questions:

1 How are we doing financially? (Lagging indicator of performance.)

2 How are we doing in the marketplace? (Current indicator of performance.)

3 How are we doing internally: staff, operations, quality? (Current indicator of performance.)

4 What's new: tests, pilots, research, key projects? (Future indicator of performance.)

At this point, we started a revolution. We cascaded Steve's sheet of paper down the organisation: each manager would amend it to focus on the detail of their area while ensuring they gathered data that was needed at the top. To start with, many of the sheets of paper were frighteningly blank: no one knew what was happening. Over the following month, the relevant information began to flow and management started to regain proper control over the business.

5 Changing how people behave

Cultural revolutions normally fail badly. Think of Mao Tse-tung and 50 million dead. There are good reasons why cultural revolutions fail:

- Culture change is normally an attack on the majority: culture represents the informal rules of success and survival in your organisation. Attacking the majority is not a good start. Attacking what is perceived to be at least a survivable model of behaviour does not make it any better.

- Culture change is about how people behave. Changing behaviour is an attack on people's personal behaviour. Personal attacks are not the best way to enthuse people.

- Cultural change programmes often confuse the ends and the means. The purpose of most organisations is not to produce happy employees. Happy and productive employees are a means to achieve some other end for the organisation.

- The process of cultural change often is mismanaged. It may not involve 50 million deaths, but it can involve lots of touchy-feely, introspective and interpersonal events that are highly divisive. Some people love the events and claim their lives have been transformed. Other people find they make their skin crawl.

Having trashed most cultural programmes, it is now time to praise them. In context and done well they can be essential. There are many organisations where the culture has become deeply dysfunctional. These are the organisations that turn on its head the old adage that 'organisations help ordinary people achieve extraordinary things'. There are far too many organisations that help extraordinary people achieve ordinary things.

Far too many organisations help extraordinary people achieve ordinary things.

It is mainly legacy organisations that are at risk of cultural dysfunction. They grow fat and happy. They get caught in old ways.

For a while, this does not matter. They are so strong and dominant in the market that they appear invincible. Then an upstart comes along and changes the rules of the game. The first reaction from the giant is denial. Denial continues until panic or expiration. Panic at least gives a chance of survival.

If you are tempted to start or get involved in a cultural change programme, here are a few guidelines:

- Attack culture crabwise: from the side on. Focus your overt efforts on the business goal, which most people can rally behind. To achieve that goal, you will need to put in place a number of enabling activities, which will include rewards, measures, how we work, skills and more. Behaviours are embedded in this.

- Be relentlessly positive. Celebrate all the right behaviours. If a shop assistant gives a disgruntled shopper a refund, celebrate the assistant's initiative and customer focus (if that is what you want to achieve). Do not attack everyone else for lack of initiative or customer focus. Slowly, people will get the message about what is valued in the organisation.

- Use cultural change levers. Reward and measurement systems are very powerful at driving behaviour. If the rewards are 100 per cent commission, do not be surprised if you have a high-performing and low-ethics sales force.

- Lead from the front. People will listen politely to speeches about culture, because they have to. Round the coffee machine they will quickly decide whether the speech was rhetoric or reality. To make it real, you have to support your words with decisions, especially tough decisions.

Values into action

The new head teacher wanted to instil a sense of respect for the individual. The leadership team talked this through and liked the idea, but no one really knew what it meant. Then one day a classroom teacher gave a whole class detention because one individual stole something, and no one owned up. The head teacher asked how a whole class detention showed respect for the individual. There were no more whole class detentions after that.

Meanwhile, the PE teacher had a real reputation for pushing the pupils. She seemed to believe in ritual humiliation of the fat and the asthmatic. That was not respect for the individual either. The PE teacher would not budge on her standards. She soon decided to leave, and they brought in another PE teacher who helped all the pupils, not just the fittest.

Slowly, the culture of the school changed. There was no one great breakthrough event, no need for the transformative conference dealing with personal and interpersonal behaviour. Instead, all the staff learned together what they really meant by respect for the individual. Because they felt they owned the journey, rather than it being dictated to them, they backed it and it worked.

4.5 Making things happen: managing projects

Most battles are won and lost before the first shot is fired. The same is true of most business battles. Make sure you are set up for success before you embark on a new challenge. It is far better to spend one month playing hard ball over the set-up of a project than to spend 12 months of misery trying to deliver an outcome that was impossible from the outset. The high PQ manager instinctively will invest very heavily in setting up an agenda for success; the naive manager will accept a challenge out of duty and commitment. A year later, the high PQ manager will be seen to be a success, and the diligent but naive manager will be seen to be a failure.

> Most battles are won and lost before the first shot is fired.

The simplest way to run a complicated project is, in theory, to hire a great project manager. You can find plenty of people with PRINCE2 qualifications (**PR**ojects **IN** Controlled Environments, a de facto process-based method for effective project management), who know all about Gantt or PERT charts, risk and issue logs and critical paths. This is good technical knowledge to have at your disposal and should ensure that the most obvious disasters are avoided.

Your first job as manager is not to run the detail of the process. Like change management, your first job is to make sure that your project is set up to succeed. You are likely to succeed if you:

● work on the right problem

● find the right sponsor

● hire the right team

● have the right process.

In other words, the requirements for success are the same for project management as they are for change management. But the challenges of the project management process are different from the challenges of change management. Because they are so important, we will remind ourselves briefly about the need for the right problem, sponsor and team, and then we will focus on the right process for project management.

Work on the right problem

The right answer to the wrong problem is worthless. A good test of your problem is to ask, 'Who owns this problem? Who cares enough about it to act on it?'

If no one in top management is interested in the challenge you want to work on, then you will get little support and you will find it hard to make any progress. In contrast, if you are working on something directly for the CEO, suddenly you will find things are much easier: busy executives suddenly will find gaps in their diary to meet you; you will be able to recruit the A team to help you and you will find that budget mysteriously becomes available.

Find the right sponsor

From your point of view, a good sponsor will have four qualities:

1 **Political power**: they can fix things and make things happen.

2 **Credibility**: they will have a track record of making things happen.

3 **Personal stake in the game**: your project needs to be important to them. Altruism is not enough: when the going gets tough you need them to support you, not walk away.

4 **Trustworthiness**: you need to be confident that they will deliver on what they say.

The CEO is often a great sponsor. CEO projects are never allowed to fail; you get support, budget and visibility. And the job of the sponsor is not to run the project: that is your job. The right sponsor will help ensure you set the project up for success with the right team and budget and will be on hand to lend support at critical moments: when you hit turbulence or when you have a major milestone to report back on.

Hire the right team

A poor team will make mountains out of molehills; a good team will make molehills out of mountains. From the manager's perspective, this is the difference between failure and success and heaven and hell. Always hold out for the A team who, by definition, already will be busy elsewhere.

The right team will have the right mix of skills. But they will also have the right values: initiative, drive, people focus and resilience. In the words of one CEO: 'I hire most people for their technical skills and fire most for their [lack of] values and people skills.'

The right values are the least used selection criteria, often with catastrophic results. If you have a high-performing, action-focused, risk-taking team and you bring in a cautious, negative, analytically focused sort of person, then it does not matter how good their technical skills are: you will create an unhappy and underperforming team fairly quickly.

Have the right process

There is a whole industry dedicated to project management. Fortunately, you do not need to master the 40 separate activities and 7 main processes of PRINCE2 project management to manage a project. If you happen to be building a nuclear power station next week, then certainly you will need your risk logs, issue logs, meeting logs, activity logs, master logs, mitigating actions and massive PERT or Gantt chart. But the chances are that your project will be slightly simpler than building a nuclear power station. And, if you need project management expertise, then there are plenty of fully qualified project managers who can assist you. As a manager, you do not need to do everything yourself; you have to find the right people to do it for you.

In practice, you will find that the wrong process is the least dangerous of the four horsemen of the apocalypse. If you have the right problem, the right godfather and the right team, then, even if you start out with the wrong process, you will have the will and skill to change course, as necessary.

Good project management is not about making things complicated, it is about making things simple. You can do this by starting at the end: focus on what the outcome should be, how you will measure it and how you will know when you have succeeded. Be specific, because that drives clarity and focus for you and your team.

Once you have the right end in mind, work out the minimum number of steps required to get there. This is a simple critical path. For product innovation, it might look like this: research the opportunity/market; design the product; make it; sell it; ship it; invoice. Then you can start driving down into detail on each part of the critical path. But keep sight of the big picture so that you can focus on what matters. You need to deal with all the day-to-day detail, but do not get lost in the detail.

Alongside this critical path, you need an effective governance process. Set this up the right way. Some governance processes resemble the Spanish Inquisition. You have to go and prove your innocence to sceptical senior managers. They get involved only at update time, which means that they need extensive briefing, and they will be ever anxious that they do not really know what is going on. So, they ask for more detail and make more challenges. This is an old world command and control way of doing things, and it does not help you. It means you spend as much time preparing reports as you do working on the project itself.

Instead of the traditional reporting relationship, set up a steering committee with the brief that it will act as an advisory group. They are not there to control, but to advise and support. Instead of having a group of semi-detached senior managers, bring on board a group of key stakeholders who have some skin in the game. They should have an interest in seeing your project succeed. Even groups like finance have an interest in your success: if they validated the financial numbers you presented to size the prize at the start of the project, they will want to know that their work remains relevant and respected. You want natural supporters on your steering committee, but you also want to co-opt onto your steering committee potential sources of trouble. Finance, if not involved, can cause problems: if they are involved, you will hear of their concerns early and you will be able to work with them to resolve them.

How to manage projects

1 **Start at the end**

   Be clear about the desired outcome, build a business case, size the prize, and quantify the opportunity.

2 **Answer the right question**

   Understand what problem or opportunity you are addressing, make sure it is important, urgent and relevant.

3 Work for the right client

Ensure that the problem or opportunity has an owner who wants it addressed, and that the owner will back you and has the power to get the right staff and budget for you.

4 Build your coalition

Identify the key stakeholders who can help or hinder the project, understand their needs and expectations and get their active support.

5 Recruit the A team

Make sure that you have the best talent on your team. If you can secure only the B team, ask whether your project is genuinely important to important people.

6 Simplify the task

Break down the project into small, short and simple steps that anyone can follow and accomplish.

7 Sequence the tasks

Understand dependencies: what needs to happen before what? Create a timetable with clear deadlines and milestones that you can track and that ensure the dependencies are met.

8 Monitor effectively

Put in place the right governance: ensure key stakeholders are involved and supportive; have regular updates in advance of each key deadline so corrective action can be taken promptly. Avoid over-monitoring and paralysis through analysis.

9 Manage the key risks, issues and obstacles

Identify remedial actions for the top challenges. Avoid creating a bureaucracy of risk logs and issue logs that cover every known risk to mankind.

10 Start now

Drive to action. Find some early wins and communicate them; demonstrate progress and build your bandwagon of support.

4.6 The art of unreasonable management: ruthlessness

Perhaps, in a perfect world, managers would always be reasonable. We do not live in a perfect world and managers are not always reasonable. The best managers are selectively unreasonable and ruthless. The worst managers are always unreasonable and ruthless. Being ruthless is not the same as being a bully, showing aggression, personalising issues and making life a misery for everyone. There are plenty of people out there who are like that. They are collecting enemies who will be only too pleased to see them fail and to help them fail when the time comes.

> The best managers are selectively unreasonable and ruthless.

If you ask senior leaders if they are ruthless, they will nearly always deny it. They do not like to see themselves that way. But look at how they behave and they are ruthless when they have to be (see the box below). Even if they will not admit to being ruthless, they will admit to having a hard edge. Spot the difference, if you can.

To be effective, you need to know when to be ruthless (and when not), and how to be ruthless.

Ruthless or hard edged?

Penicillin was discovered by Alexander Fleming between the two World Wars. But it had proven very hard to manufacture in large batches. Eventually, during the Second World War, large batches started to be produced.

One early batch found its way to North Africa, where the British were fighting the Germans. The British generals were unsure how best to use the new wonder medicine. There were wounded soldiers who would need large amounts of penicillin: even so, some might die anyway and others might have survived without the drug. They could not tell in advance. And then there were the soldiers who had caught the clap in the pleasure palaces of Cairo and Alexandria. It would not take much penicillin to sort them out, but they were hardly worthy causes.

They sent a message back to London asking Churchill for advice.

What would you do: save the soldiers who had been fighting, or save the soldiers who had been fooling around?

Churchill's reply was clear: use the drug for 'best military advantage'; get as many soldiers back fighting as soon as possible. The pleasure palaces were emptied and the wounded heroes were left to take their chances.

Success does not always come from being nice.

When to be unreasonable and ruthless

Sun Tzu's three rules of warfare make a useful reappearance at this stage. Only fight (be unreasonable and ruthless) when there is:

- a prize worth fighting for
- certainty of success
- no other way of winning the prize.

The times it is worth being ruthless are when the stakes are highest. This means:

- budget negotiations
- target setting
- team formation
- assignments and promotions.

To make this simple: if you work on the right assignment with a great team and a good budget to meet sensible targets, you have won 80 per cent of the battle. If you are on the wrong assignment with a lousy team, a thin budget and absurd targets, start looking for another job. There may be other battles you need to fight, but do not waste personal time and equity on fighting skirmishes: even if you win the skirmish, you will lose a friend, and you could pay for that dearly when the big battles start. If you see a skirmish, make your position clear and then concede, preferably by negotiating for something in return for your concession.

How to be unreasonable and ruthless

Great things are rarely achieved by reasonable people. Look at the heroes of history and you will not find many reasonable people among them: from Charlemagne to Churchill, Genghis Khan to Kennedy, you find events shaped by people who achieved the impossible. The great entrepreneurs from Getty to Gates are not modest people who settled for a reasonable outcome: they played to win and to win big. In your own organisation, you can probably identify people who achieve much: they may well be among the more ruthless and unreasonable managers in the organisation. Meanwhile, many reasonable and decent managers find themselves side-lined.

It is possible to be ruthless without being unpleasant. The key is to understand that you can be unreasonable and ruthless about the outcomes, while still being reasonable about the method of getting there. The following examples are where you need to find your hard edge:

Budget negotiations

Be very clear about the acceptable goals and why they are acceptable. Then stick limpet-like to that position. If you concede anything, negotiate for something in return. Be very clear about the consequences and risks of any change. Make any deviation from your position feel very risky.

> If you concede anything, negotiate for something in return.

Set expectations early: anchor the discussion at the right level before the formal budget round starts (see section 2.7: Setting budgets: the politics of performance in Chapter 2).

Use both the formal and informal processes to make your stand. Do not rely on the formal staff process to deliver the outcome you want: lobby hard with key decision makers behind the scenes. Make sure you have a story to sell them: the decision makers are going to back you, a story, the numbers and their staff, in roughly that order of priority. If you have credibility and a good story, you should be able to sell the outcome you need.

Target setting

This is the mirror image of budget negotiations, and the same principles apply. Always set one against the other: a change in budget should be mirrored by a change in targets.

If you are setting the targets for your team, the same rules apply but with the intent of achieving the opposite outcome: to set the most stretching goals possible without actually breaking the team.

Team formation

Always hold out for the A team. Typically, new assignments are staffed with the untried and untested, together with a few who have been tested and found wanting.

Go round the formal assignment process. Sell your assignment to individuals you want on your team. Build their enthusiasm; help them identify a way out of their current responsibilities. Spot the good people who are frustrated by their current managers and cultivate them, even if you do not need them right away. When you do need them, it will be much easier if you already have a good relationship with them and they trust you.

Move people on. This does not have to be unpleasant. Do not focus on why someone messed up. Focus on what they can do well, and where their talents are best used (elsewhere). Keep looking around the organisation to see if there is a slot that they could fill (where you can move the person). Focusing on the positives is good for the individual and also means that you can move them on faster and with less conflict than if you focus on the negatives.

Assignments and promotions

Work your networks. Find out where and when the interesting assignments are emerging. In many cases, early stage initiatives have minimal budget and depend on voluntary effort to scope them. Volunteer your time. Scope the initiative to suit your needs. If you like the outcome, you will be in a prime position to have the role in the initiative that you designed for yourself. Let your future potential boss know how excited you are at the prospect of working for them. Equally, make yourself highly unavailable and over-committed on essential work, if there is a nightmare assignment coming up.

Find a sponsor. A quick way to the top is to hang on to the coat-tails of a high-flying executive: they all need a team they can trust and depend on. If you are smart, you will have more than one sponsor so that you are not left high and dry if your main sponsor blows up or leaves the organisation. Volunteering to do interesting odd jobs in your spare time is a quick way to get noticed and appreciated by senior executives.

Set career expectations with your boss at an early stage, and then keep on reinforcing your claim. The essential discussion is called 'What do I have to do to get promoted?' Bosses hate being cornered this way, but the conversation helps by:

- clarifying what may be ambiguous
- forcing the boss to take your career prospects seriously
- making it difficult for the boss to avoid putting you up for promotion when the time is right.

4.7 Managing your boss: and difficult people

In the new world of flat organisations, you will have to work with people who have far more power and influence than you do. You have to find a way of influencing them positively.

Perhaps the most important power person for you to manage is your boss. Bosses are problematic. You will never find an instruction model for your boss, and when things break down it will always be your fault. You have little power over your boss, but your boss has plenty of power over you. In other words, they are the perfect practice ground for developing your influencing skills. If you can influence your boss well, you can influence other powerful people as well.

In this section we will look at how you can:

- manage your boss
- say no to your boss (or any other powerful person)
- manage an unreasonable boss
- deal with unreasonable people
- influence very senior people.

How to manage your boss

We all land up on the wrong side of a boss at some stage of our careers. It is not a pleasant experience. It does not matter that the boss may be at fault: the boss has the power and we have the problem. The good news is that if you learn to manage your boss, over whom you have little power, you will have learned to manage your boss, over whom you have little power, you will have learned the basics of managing almost anyone.

> The boss has the power and we have the problem.

A good starting point is to see the world through the eyes of your boss. If you have a team, consider what you look for from your team members. The chances are that your boss is looking for roughly the same things from you. Here is what bosses typically say that they want from their teams:

- reliability
- honesty and loyalty
- initiative
- hard work.

These are low hurdles, over which many people fall.

The basic principles of managing your boss are simple:

- **Reliability**. You have to deliver good performance. No matter how smart you are in terms of PQ, if you have a gold medal in incompetence, nothing can save you. Good career management is about substance as well as style.

  Set expectations well and over-communicate. This is the other side of reliability. Reliability is not just about delivering on expectations: it is also about managing expectations. No boss will really understand what you are capable of. They will not know what an acceptable workload is, because the nature of most work is highly ambiguous in today's organisations. You have to tell the boss what you can do, what you cannot do, when you need help and when you are being overworked or underworked. Set these expectations early so that there are no surprises for the boss: bosses hate surprises, which are rarely good. If things are going wrong, flag the problem early so that remedial action can be taken and the drama does not turn into a crisis.

- **Be loyal**. Most bosses are reasonably forgiving. They know that things go wrong. Although many sins are forgivable, disloyalty is not one of them. When a boss stops trusting a team member, it is simply a question of time before the team member is moved on. Disloyalty is not just about trying to stab your boss in the back: it is about failing to support the boss at awkward moments, bad-mouthing the boss and showing that you are less than committed. It can be painful to be loyal, but it is essential to career survival. The essence of loyalty is trust. We will see the trust equation later, which states that trust is a function of alignment (do we share the same values and priorities?) and credibility (can you deliver on what you say?). Once you have a bond of trust, any manager will want to keep you on the team.

- **Initiative**. Be positive. Bosses have enough problems of their own without you adding to the list. When there are problems and challenges, raise them with the boss but offer a solution at the same time. Even if it is not the best solution, the boss will appreciate working with someone who brings solutions, not just problems.

- **Hard work**. Bosses know who puts in the extra effort and who does not. And not all work is glamorous. The day-to-day graft of management can be tedious. You help your boss not only by doing the glamorous things, but also by dealing with the rubbish so that your boss is freed to do other things.

- **Adapt to the style of the boss**. If your boss has a style you dislike, that is your problem and not the boss's. You have to find ways of working with the style of the boss. If your boss likes detail, hates risk, wants frequent updates and is best early in the morning, then set the alarm clock for an early rise and work to his or her needs. If your boss is hands off, big picture, goal-focused and is best in the early evening, you have a wonderful chance to learn about a different working style.

How to say no to your boss

You must be able to say no to your boss if you are to have any control over your own destiny. If you cannot say no, then you are at the mercy of the whims and judgement of your boss. If your boss is benign and also has good judgement, you will find yourself working on the right agenda and the right problem. But saying no is not a risk that always pays off over a long career. It is an art form that has to be learned.

Saying no to your boss is harder than resisting ideas from elsewhere in the organisation. It is harder to ignore your boss than it is to ignore your colleagues. If you are close to your boss, it pays to be direct: say no and explain why, in terms the boss understands so that he or she realises that it is in his or her own best interests not to proceed. As you do this, be clear about the risks

> It pays to be positive, particularly with a negative message.

and consequences of proceeding, but also try to come up with an alternative. It pays to be positive, particularly with a negative message. You need to offer solutions, not just problems.

So you need to deal with the issue, and with the boss. The challenge of this game is to find ways of saying no without actually saying no. Risking alliterative overload, remember the three Ps of saying no: priorities, process and people.

Priorities

The priorities argument buys time without forcing you to oppose the idea. It forces your boss to think through the consequences of starting something new (something else will have to take a back seat) and will force some uncomfortable choices about what is most important and urgent. Even if you support the idea completely, you should still have this discussion. Typically, the priorities discussion will kick off with one of two questions:

1 How does this fit with my other priorities? Which ones would you like me to put back/defer for this idea?

2 Should we do this before or after X episode (which is more urgent and/or on the critical path)?

Process

The process discussion can also be very positive. This is where you can show you are thinking about solutions, not just problems. At the same time, you are still forcing discussion about possible risks, consequences and alternatives. This is a discussion that can slowly turn a bad idea into a good one. A good process discussion often will start with:

● Could we do it another way instead? (Better, faster, cheaper, less risky.)

● How can we set this up for success? (People, budget, time: connects to priorities.) Negotiate hard on this. The outcome should either be that the idea is dropped, or it is set up for success. If it is set for success, you may want to take the idea up yourself.

People

This is a discussion about fit: are you the right fit for the project? It is a discussion you do not want to have too often with a boss, who will start to doubt whether you are fit for anything. But it is often an elegant way of avoiding a direct attack on the idea and can work well if you have an alternative in mind. A neat way of doing this is to suggest that someone else take the lead, but you will find time to help, support and direct the other person, as necessary. This takes you out of the firing line without being seen to be unsupportive. The questions to raise are:

- Who would be ideal to lead this?
- How best can I support this? In what role (preferably not leading it)?

How to manage an unreasonable boss

Ruthless people are not necessarily bad. As we have seen, all leaders need to be ruthless at some point.

It pays to separate out style and substance in a ruthless boss. Normally, you will find this leads to one of two types of ruthlessness: bosses who are ruthless in achieving their personal goals; bosses who are ruthless about achieving the goals of the organisation. Both can be uncomfortable to work with. It pays to know which sort of ruthless person you are working with.

Effectively unreasonable for the organisation	Painfully unreasonable for self
Fights selectively: big battles	Fights on everything
Inflexible about outcomes, flexible on means	Inflexible on ends and means: 'My way or no way'

▶

Effectively unreasonable for the organisation	Painfully unreasonable for self
Focuses on business imperatives	Personalises issues and challenges
Future-focused, creates win/wins	Creates blame culture, win/lose
Stretches people: climate of opportunity	Breaks people: climate of fear
Total commitment given and returned	Total commitment expected but not returned
Total persistence in chasing a goal: high trust	Chops and changes to suit personal needs
Ambitious for organisation and self	Ambitious for self

Managing the effectively unreasonable manager

Reasonable managers are often easy to work with. They set reasonable goals and expect you to comply with the process. Provided you do not mess up, you will be fine. Unreasonable bosses have much higher expectations. They will want to achieve more, they will stretch you and the team. But they will be flexible about how you get there: process compliance is not high on their list of priorities and they are more likely to forgive you if you mess up occasionally, provided they believe you are still capable of stretching to top performance.

If you work for such a boss, you need to follow all the standard rules of managing your boss that have already been outlined. In addition, you will need to deliver against a much higher performance bar. This is good news in that it will stretch you, and you will learn and grow. And your boss should, normally, be supportive.

Your challenge is to decide if this is a boss who you can trust when it comes to bonus and promotions. You will have put in extra, discretionary, effort; you will have learned and grown: will you be rewarded or taken for granted? To help you decide, it pays to watch the feet, not the mouth. Look at the track record of your boss, not at what he or she says. If your boss has a good track record of supporting team members at crunch time, you can trust what is said. If your boss is more focused on the mission than on the team, take care. You may enjoy learning and being stretched, but your career will not thrive. Keep a look out for another boss who can help you more. How you do this is covered in section 4.8: Managing your career: career is a noun and a verb.

Managing the painfully unreasonable boss

These people are often the power barons where you work. They create their own little fiefdoms. Either you are part of the team, or you are part of the enemy. And, if you are part of the team, you have to be 100 per cent loyal and committed to the power baron.

The simplest way of dealing with such people is to sell your soul to the devil: sign up with the power baron and live life on his or her own terms. Power barons need loyal retainers and, if you are one of them, you can go far by following the baron. But, if you sign up, you need to judge whether the baron is likely to be successful and trustworthy. If you think that they may not succeed, that they may jump ship, or you do not trust them, then you face some uncomfortable choices.

In the short term, you have to live with the devil. It is no use getting sucked into negative emotions of anger, frustration and depression. Your performance will suffer and your nightmare boss will become even worse. You land up in a vicious circle that ends only with the exit door. Remember, your first goal is to survive.

> Your first goal is to survive.

You can then either outlast the boss, or buy time to make a graceful exit to another boss, department or organisation on terms you dictate. Some simple survival mechanisms for living with such a boss include:

- **Loyalty**. Disloyalty is the greatest cardinal sin for all managers. It breaks the bond of trust. Loyalty means always backing the boss, even on unpopular decisions. It means no bad-mouthing in private: word will get back to the boss eventually, and then you are finished.

- **Flattery**. Devils have huge egos that need constant massaging. Convince the devils that you are a loyal follower and want to learn their dark secrets. They may look after you well, until they decide to dump you.

- **Do not take it personally**. However offensive the devil is personally, do not take it that way. Focus on solutions, actions and the future personally and with the boss. Change the devil's agenda to a focus on action, solutions and the future by relentless role modelling.

- **Sit it out**. The corporate carousel moves round fairly fast. Few bosses last more than one or two years. You can learn much from all bosses, even if all the lessons are negative.

- **Prepare your escape route**. Find other sponsors in the organisation; find other opportunities and go for them at the right time. Explain to your devil boss that you are simply seeking the right personal development opportunities and experience: pretend you like working for the devil boss; you simply need new experiences.

How to deal with unreasonable people

Organisations are not always happy families; even families are not always happy families. You will come across colleagues who think politics is all about back stabbing, positioning, making other people look bad and ruthlessly promoting themselves at all times. They will deceive happily in order to get their way and, because they deceive often, they become very good at it. They appear to lack any moral compass or conscience. They are sociopaths. Estimates vary, but up to 5 per cent of staff may have some degree of sociopathic leanings. That is a small proportion, but they can have a disproportionate effect on the organisation and on you.

When faced with aggression, it is very easy to respond emotionally. If you do this, you will lose. If you fight aggression with aggression, you are fighting on their terms. They have more experience of fighting that way, and will win. If you flee, you become another of their victims and you lose again. So, you cannot fight and you cannot flee: what can you do?

The first step is to take control of your own reactions. Remember, you always have a choice about how you feel and how you react. If someone is being annoying and offensive, you have every right to feel angry and upset. But there is no law that says you must feel angry and upset: that is a choice you make.

If you focus on their behaviour, it is hard not to react emotionally. Instead, you can choose to focus on the task and the issue. This may well annoy them, because you are not playing their game: they want to distract you away from one issue onto other issues. If you remain positive and professional, this will also annoy them: that is not the reaction they enjoy. Role model good behaviour and focus on the core issue. This is your territory, the territory of professional management. Stick to this and the sociopath will find life hard.

The different approaches are summarised in the table below. Remember that you have a choice about how you react: choose well.

Choose your approach

	Passive victim	Assertive leader	Aggressive sociopath
Characteristics	Allow others to choose for you; inhibited, set up to lose	Choose for self; honest, self-respecting, find the win-win	Choose for others; tactless, self-enhancing; play to win, others to lose
Your own feelings	Anxious, ignored, manipulated	Confident, self-respecting, goal-focused	Superior, deprecatory, controlling
How you make others feel	Guilty or superior: frustrated with you	Valued and respected	Humiliated and resentful
How you are seen	Lack of respect; do not know where you stand	Respect; know where you stand	Vengeful, fearful, angry, distrustful
Outcome	Lose at your expense	Negotiated win/win	You win at others' expense

How to influence very senior people

When dealing with very senior people, it is easy to get altitude sickness: a shortness of breath, headaches and a general feeling of nausea and disorientation. The consequences can be fatal to your career. These feelings are wholly unnecessary.

● **See the world through their eyes**. Senior people need you. You have some idea, analysis or plan that might help them. Make sure that your idea is big enough to interest them, or at least it fits with a big agenda that they are chasing. Do your research and get advice beforehand: find out what their agenda is and how you can fit in. If you have a plan for reducing the consumption of paper clips, do not expect to find much excitement for your plan from senior people: they have other things to worry about. It pays to be bold.

● **Be positive, even enthusiastic**. In some organisations, enthusiasm is regarded as a certifiable psychiatric disorder. But, equally, most organisations and most people have no defence against enthusiasm, which is infectious. If you are enthusiastic about your idea, others will tend to believe your idea must be good. If you are not enthusiastic about your idea, do not expect anyone to be enthusiastic on your behalf. In a world where senior people are used to dealing with problems, it is a breath of fresh air to find an enthusiastic and positive person bringing solutions and ideas. You will be judged as much by how you appear as by what you say, so make appearances count in the way you act as well as the way you dress.

● **Act as their partner**. If you act like a junior, you will be treated like a junior. All hierarchies are set up as a series of parent–child relationships, which is fine for the people in the parent role. But adults do not like being treated as children, which is one of the reasons so many workplaces are dysfunctional. Act like an adult partner: you have something they need. Even if you are pitching for investment, you still have something they need: you have a great investment and they are fortunate that you are bringing it to them. You are not a supplicant, supplier, junior or child in the relationship: you are their partner, so act that way.

- **Master your brief**. The more you have mastered your brief, the more confident and relaxed you will be. Mastery is more than mastering all the detail. Mastery means knowing what the senior people really want, what their big picture is and where you fit into it, and what sorts of questions they will ask. They will focus on the big issues, not the detail. If you focus only on the detail, you are likely to be wrong footed by questions about the big picture.

- **Be prepared**. You never know when you might bump into a senior person. You can then chat about the weather, if you want. But, if you are prepared, you can engage them in an impromptu, but substantive, discussion about your agenda (see the box below).

The Fairy Queen strikes

I was working on a toilet soap called Zest, minding my own business. Suddenly, a shadow loomed over me. It was the CEO. He was on one of his royal visits: he was doing a walk around to see how people in marketing were doing. So, he asked how I was doing, and I muttered something about nothing. He moved to the next cubicle that was occupied by the manager of my rival, Fairy Toilet Soap.

The CEO asked the manager of Fairy how she was doing. She perked up and said, 'Well, Jurgen, I am really pleased you've come by, because I was looking for some advice on this new promotion we are planning...' Jurgen, the CEO, was delighted to help the Fairy Queen: he had started life in marketing and was keen to show he still knew his stuff.

Following the CEO's visit, the Fairy Queen got her controversial new promotion approved by all the departments in record time: no one was going to oppose the CEO. Months later, my more modest idea was still battling its way through the system. The Fairy Queen had used the CEO as a partner, not a boss, and was ready to strike when he came.

Act like a partner and be ready to strike when dealing with senior people.

4.8 Managing your career: career is a noun and a verb

For some people career is a noun: it describes a steady progression from bright eyed graduate to the point of retiring where a grateful employer gives you a carriage clock for 40 years of loyal service. For others, it is a verb that describes a roller coaster of experience as you move between roles and employers: the highs are high, the lows are low and there is no carriage clock, but there are a lot of memories.

Whether you choose to have a career or to career through life, you still need to manage your journey. Even the best managers can be lousy at managing their own career: they are then frustrated when less accomplished colleagues pass them by on the up escalator to the top. With a little PQ, you can manage your career well. Career management is not a substitute for good performance; it is a way of ensuring you are recognised for good performance.

> Career management is not a substitute for good performance; it is a way of ensuring you are recognised for good performance.

The box below summarises how you can manage your career, or how to career, successfully:

Manage your career

- Find your calling: you excel only at what you enjoy.
- Find the right organisation: winning and values.
- Find the right role: go where the opportunity is.
- Find the right boss: avoid the Death Stars.
- Find the right assignments: play to your strengths.
- Build your network: always have a plan B.
- Build your skills: never stop learning.

- Build your claim to fame: and then stake your claim.
- Act the part: and then be the part.
- Control your destiny: or someone else will.

This section explores each of these themes in a little more detail.

Find your calling

Management is hard work. Occasionally, it can be exciting, exhilarating and even terrifying. But often it is dull. We can all sustain a high level of effort for a few weeks or even months when there is a real crunch. But a career is a marathon, not a sprint. You have to sustain high levels of effort for decades, not for days. You have to keep on putting in discretionary effort. You can do this only if you enjoy what you do.

The words enjoy and work rarely go together. The whole work–life balance industry is based on the implicit premise that work is not enjoyable and should be reduced: when did you last hear a work–life balance guru advocating more work?

Enjoying work is not like social enjoyment. It is about finding fulfilment and satisfaction in the work itself. An easy test is to see how fast time passes. When we are bored, an hour stretches to eternity. When we are deeply engrossed in something, time flies past. When we lose ourselves in our work, we are on the way to finding meaning and satisfaction in what we do. This sense of fulfilment does not have to come from changing the world. Look at craftsmen working: they often concentrate so hard on what they are doing that the outside world disappears for them. Whatever your calling may be, find it.

In working with and interviewing senior leaders, I often hear them complain about how hard they work, the late evenings and the long travel. But it is a façade: it is their way of showing off. Listen harder, and you find they enjoy every minute of their time. Their greatest fear is retirement: that is when they lose meaning and purpose. It is the same with top sports people. They may complain about the long hours and the endless, tedious, training. But there is nothing else in the world that they would rather do.

Of course, it takes effort to reach the top and to be your best. You can do these things only if you enjoy them. You excel only at what you enjoy, so find what you enjoy.

Find the right organisation

Just as there is no such thing as the perfect leader, so there is no such thing as the perfect organisation. You always have to make some trade-offs. And, to make things harder, you never really know what you are letting yourself in for until it is too late. Any employer likes to present its best face to the world: you discover reality only when you have joined. The grass always looks greener on the other side of the hill. So, remember that it is greenest where it rains the most. You cannot have it all.

You can tilt the odds in your favour by knowing what to look for:

- Will this firm grow or fail?
- Will I acquire useful skills?
- Will my track record be recognised?
- Is it the right culture for me?

Note that pay is not on the list. If you make a decision about your career based on 10 per cent here or there next year, you are focusing on the wrong issue. If pay counts, take the long-term view and ask: 'How can I be earning ten times this amount in (say) ten years' time?' That gives you a better test of the opportunities that lie ahead and what you will have to do to succeed. If there is no chance of real income progression, then 10 per cent extra today does not help you very much at all.

Will the firm grow or fail?

Let us pretend you have a choice: you can join firm X, which has a declining share in a declining market, or company Y, which is a growing firm in a growing market. It should not take you long to work out which firm to join, all other things (like pay) being equal. Where there is growth, there is opportunity: where there is decline there is risk. Do your strategic analysis on the firm: has it got a source of unfair competitive advantage? Is it in a growing industry? Look past the PR bluster of the firm and make your own decision about its prospects. Do your independent research: ask people who have worked there, or in the industry, about the firm; look for industry and media reports. There is plenty of independent advice out there, when you look for it.

Will I acquire useful skills?

Career security no longer comes from your loyal employer; it comes from your employability. If you have the right skills, and keep them up to date, you will be in demand and you can progress your career. Without the right skills, you become dependent on the goodwill of your employer. That is an increasingly uncomfortable place to be.

Ask yourself not only, 'Do I have the skills to succeed in this organisation?'; ask yourself, 'Will I be acquiring the skills that set me up for the next stage of my career, for my next promotion?' Your skills define your prospects, so make sure you have the chance to grow your skills for the future, as well as using your existing skills for the present.

Will my track record be recognised?

If you join ACME widgets and do great things for them, you can rightly be proud of what you have done. But you may have some difficulty convincing a future employer, who has never heard of ACME widgets, that you have done great things. In contrast, if you join Goldman Sachs, McKinsey or P&G, immediately you get star rating on your CV. You will find it easy to sell any minor accomplishments there to a future employer, who will be more than happy to buy in some star dust from a top employer.

Inevitably, there is a sting in the tail. Gold-standard employers may burnish your CV but, once you have left the gold standard, it is very hard to return to it. You can cash your chips only once, so make sure that you cash them in at the right time for the right reason.

Is it the right culture for me?

Warren Buffett once said, 'I find that when a manager with a great reputation joins a firm with a lousy reputation, it is the reputation of the firm which remains intact.' Do not expect to change the culture of the firm you join. I was asked to join a machine bureaucracy to inject entrepreneurial culture into it: the machine bureaucracy remains as bureaucratic and successful as ever it was.

> You excel only at what you enjoy, so make sure you find a place of work that you can enjoy.

This returns us to the theme of enjoyment: you excel only at what you enjoy, so make sure you find a place of work that you can enjoy.

That is partly about the work itself, but it is also about the sorts of people you will work with.

Again, do your research. Talk to people who have worked at the firm previously and find out what they think. Do not be swayed by what the recruiters say to you: they are presenting their best face to you. And, even if you meet your potential line manager, recognise that line managers come and go.

Find the right role

Clearly, the right role has to be one that you enjoy and that plays to your strengths. But, it also needs to be a role that will let you grow your career. This leads you in two opposite directions:

● Go to the heart of power: at head office you have access and visibility with all the power players, but it is hard to stand out. Power attracts talent like honey attracts bees: you will be in the middle of intense competition.

- Go to an outpost of empire: here you have freedom to experiment, grow yourself and create a claim to fame. But, you will be out of the power and communications loops, unless you are careful.

Here is how to manage the trade-offs.

Power at the heart of empire

Being at the heart of empire confers huge advantages to the manager, including:

- access to informal information and knowledge
- access to key decision makers, informally and frequently
- ability to build an extended network of managers with power
- early sight of attractive programmes and positions
- visibility to senior executives
- insight into the organisation's real priorities and decision-making processes.

None of these insider advantages comes gift-wrapped, waiting for you at your cubicle the day you arrive at head office. You have to work to build the informal networks and knowledge. But, at least you have the opportunity to build these informal networks faster than someone in the outposts of empire who visits head office only once a quarter for a conference or an appraisal.

A cubicle in head office does not guarantee success. There are some functions and roles that carry more weight than others. In career terms, it makes sense to be where the power is. This varies by organisation, for instance:

- Procter & Gamble (P&G): marketing
- GM and Ford: finance
- Dyson: design
- professional service firms: clients
- Toyota and Nissan: engineering.

A finance person at P&G's Cincinnati head office or a marketing person at Ford's Dearborn headquarters will be close to power, but they will not have it. They will be like the beggar looking through the shop windows on Fifth Avenue: they are close to wealth, they can see the wealth, but they cannot touch the wealth. It is a frustrating experience. Power starts by making the right career choices. Some organisations deliberately cultivate future leaders by placing them at the heart of power early in their careers. BP selects high-potential graduates to work in the CEO's office for one or two years. In that time, they will learn how the organisation really works; they will build their networks of support and influence and they will start to learn how a senior executive thinks and acts. These are invaluable lessons to learn. But gaining this sort of access is unusual.

The main drawback to seeking the heart of power is competition. Your colleagues are your deadliest competitors. Managers are attracted to power like moths to a light. A short walk around any corporate headquarters is enough to find managers dancing around different light and power sources, all trying to get as close as possible to the brightest light. Inevitably, quite a few get burned in the process. In a moment, we will look at how to acquire the power once you have identified it.

Power at the outposts of empire

Going to an outpost of empire may seem like being exiled to lingering career death. Handled incorrectly, that is exactly what it is. Handled correctly, an outpost of empire is an essential stepping stone to success.

Outposts of empire are good news. A middle manager may be lost in cubicle land at headquarters where there is intense competition for attention. Managers who know their competitive strategy will recognise that the best way to win is without a fight: occupy new territory (competitive 'white spaces' in the words of Prahalad and Hamel or Blue Ocean, if you listen to Chan Kim). These outposts often are attractive career staging posts because they:

- offer the chance to wield real authority: limited responsibility in an ambiguous matrix can be replaced by genuine authority and responsibility in an outpost

- offer rapid development: the manager can experiment – and even fail occasionally – away from the intense competition and gossip in the limelight at headquarters

- allow the manager to build a track record and build credibility. GE has many smaller business units that it calls 'lemonade stands'. These give potential general managers the chance to build and demonstrate their capabilities

- enable the manager to build a power base and an empire of his or her own: an unloved skunk works quickly can become a strategic business in its own right. IBM's PC division was an affront to an organisation that lived mainframe, but it moved quickly from being an unloved orphan to a star – until, finally, it hollowed itself out completely and got taken over by Lenovo.

An assignment to the outposts of empire can be a one-way ticket to triumph or tragedy. To avoid the latter, there are three golden rules to observe:

1 **Believe nothing**. When you negotiate your exile, you may diligently negotiate promises about what will happen on your return: the career opportunities that will be yours and the promotions available in three years' time. Anything you agree is worthless. In three years' time, the organisation will have gone through one or two reorganisations. The openings you hoped for will have disappeared into the black hole of any reorganisation. Your boss will have changed. Your new boss will not feel deeply committed to keeping promises that he did not make and that are impossible to fulfil in the new organisation anyway. You have to make your own future, rather than relying on people to keep promises made on their behalf years ago.

2   **Stay in touch.** You have to stay on the corporate radar screen. In an outpost of empire you are cut off from the gossip, the power networks, the shifting sands of new opportunities, reorganisations and new initiatives. People forget that you exist because they no longer see you in the corridor. So, make sure you find plenty of excuses to go back to the heart of empire for budget meetings, training events, corporate events. Volunteer for corporate projects that maintain your visibility and enable you to appear back in the heart of empire. Stay in touch with HR and the power brokers who will know what openings are going to appear when: make sure you manage your transition back into the corporate heart when attractive positions are opening up.

3   **Manage perceptions.** The good news about the outposts of empire is that no one in the heart of empire really understands what on earth is happening there or why. This is, of course, also the bad news. All that the functionaries back in head office see are the numbers that say whether you have positive or negative variances against budget. This makes perception management essential. It also makes it essential to set the baseline as low as possible at the start of the year, so that all the functionaries see positive variances for your unit.

Japan is different

The one-way ticket to Japan was full of promise, until I actually arrived there and found a business with no sales, no revenues and no prospect of any sales. But there were plenty of bills to be paid. No one back in New Jersey had a clue what was happening in Japan. I began to suspect that I did not have a clue, either.

Quickly, I realised there were two battles to fight:

1   Get the business going in Japan: find some revenues, fast.

2   Manage perceptions: set expectations and sell a story to our masters in New Jersey.

The story was simple: to acquire a decent business in Japan would cost at least $10 million, with all the risks of acquiring something that might not fit with our business model. We could do far better: over three years we would build a business that fitted the New Jersey business model and it would cost only $6 million, or $2 million a year.

For reasons that remain obscure, they bought the story. We had just given ourselves the licence to lose (sorry, invest) $2 million a year in the business. We had reset expectations very low, and had sold a story that our masters liked and we could deliver.

Over the next three years, we racked up enough air miles to bankrupt several airlines. Managing perceptions and staying in touch takes serious effort.

Managing a global career

1 **Do your homework**

Do your due diligence. Find out what the real state of the business is, who you will be working with, what your role will be, how much budget and authority you will have. If you do not like what you see, either negotiate or walk away from the opportunity.

2 **Work it out with your family**

This may be a great adventure for you, but not for a spouse stuck at home, unable to work and unable to communicate in the local language.

3 **Negotiate**

Far more important than pay and conditions is to set yourself up for success in terms of your role, budget and performance expectations. Play hard ball: the moment you agree to go, you lose all your negotiating power and you are committed.

4 **Do not believe any promises**

In three years' time, your new boss will be elsewhere and the organisation will have changed twice. Your new bosses will be unable, and probably unwilling, to keep promises they do not even know about. ▶

5 Understand your role

Your job is to represent the standards, knowledge and expertise of the global firm in its local context. You have to graft your global capability onto the local knowledge of the locals.

6 Re-invent yourself

In a new country, you do not carry baggage from the past. This is your chance to experiment. Take the opportunity from the start: within a month, everyone will have decided who you are in your new context. You will have acquired a new set of bags.

7 Be flexible

You will find different food, different customs, different business practices, different languages. Get out of the expat bubble and adapt to local ways. You will learn more and probably enjoy more.

8 Over-communicate

Once you have disappeared to another part of the globe, you may be forgotten. You have to manage your reputation: sell your performance and keep selling it.

9 Stay visible

Find excuses to stay involved. There are always working groups, research and initiatives that need global input and support. Find opportunities to remind the power barons that you still exist and you are doing great work.

10 Work the assignment process

In theory, HR will help. In practice, you have to help yourself. You need to spot attractive openings early and position yourself for them. You can be sure that all your colleagues at home are very happy that you are away: they will take the best pickings.

Find the right boss

Most career grief comes from having a bad boss. As a coach, this is where I find many clients struggle: how to deal with a problem boss. It is also true that many people do not leave their employer: they leave their boss. We have already looked at how you can deal with a bad boss. But the best way of dealing with a bad boss, is to make sure you have a good boss. Prevention is better than cure.

You can leave choice of your boss to the random walk of the HR and assignment system, which is called hoping to get lucky. But hope is not a method and luck is not a strategy. At minimum, you should weight the dice in your favour.

> Hope is not a method and luck is not a strategy.

In practice, everyone knows who the bad bosses are. Their reputation precedes them. And, you probably know a few bosses who you trust and want to work for. So, now you have to make sure you get picked for the right team.

First, make yourself useful to the prospective good boss. Bosses always need a helping hand with a discretionary project, an idea they are chasing, a speech they want to make, or information they are looking for. Put in some discretionary effort. Show interest in what the boss is doing; perhaps ask the boss for some advice. Engage with the boss, and role model being a great team member: positive, enthusiastic, with initiative and action focus. They will notice and, next time they are looking for a team, your name will be on their wish list.

Equally, when the Death Star bosses are looking for victims, copy Harry Potter. Put on the cloak of invisibility. Make sure you are very, very busy and completely indispensable on your existing work. The Death Star boss will pass by and look for easier victims elsewhere.

You cannot always have the boss you want. When you land up with a bad boss, do not panic. Remember that the corporate carousel keeps on turning, and no boss lasts forever. And, you can always learn, even from the bad bosses. Many of the lessons may be about how you do not want to do things yourself. But there is a reason that your boss has become a boss: there will be something that he or she does which the organisation values.

Understand that, and you will have gained one more insight about how you can succeed.

Find the right assignments

If you know the principles for finding the right organisation, role and boss, then you already know the principles for finding the right assignment. These are:

● Be proactive: do not wait to be assigned, but find what you want.

● Find something you may enjoy, with a good boss.

● Play to your strengths, and build new ones.

It is the last principle that is the tricky one. Any employer wants you to do more of what you are good at. I had one team member who did an excellent job at building a business case for an IT investment for a life insurance company. He was brilliant at it, and it led to clients signing up to multi-million investments. So he spent the next three years doing exactly the same thing for different clients. He had a claim to fame, but his career went nowhere because he became boxed in an obscure area of technical expertise. He had happily gone along with this, because he was in his comfort zone. He knew he could succeed; everyone liked what he did and he had to take no risks.

You need to play to your strengths and build your claim to fame. But you also need to be building your skills base for the future. Be prepared to stretch yourself and take some risks in doing new things, otherwise you will stagnate. Keep one eye on the present and one on the future when taking on new assignments.

The Thai tapioca test

I was coming towards the end of an assignment. Cautiously, I found out what other assignments were in the pipeline. To my horror, I found that Daniel, who liked to eat analysts for breakfast, had sold a project to do competitive analysis of the Thai tapioca market.

I was not too keen on thinly disguised industrial espionage in a language I could not speak and in an industry I did not know. And I hate tapioca. I saw a nightmare looming. I also found out that there was a Saudi marketing project. Saudi Arabia is not everyone's cup of tea and they were not going to staff it easily. But the project manager was great. So I quickly discovered unbounded enthusiasm for all things Saudi Arabian. I took the strain off the project manager by helping draft the final proposal. Meanwhile, I was mysteriously busy whenever a Thai tapioca planning session was called: my cat would die (again), or I would suddenly have an urgent meeting with my existing client. I told the Saudi project manager I wanted to work with him. He was delighted to have any sort of solution to his staffing challenge, even me.

Mysteriously, I dodged the bullet and found myself on the Saudi project, not the Thai tapioca project. Subsequent events led me to hope fervently that the Thai project was at least as bad as I had feared, but that is another story...

Build your network

Management is becoming twenty-first century slavery, with the twist that we are all volunteering to become slaves. The hype of the 24/7 society where we can have anything, any time and any place is consumer heaven. The 24/7 manager who has to do anything, any time and any place lives in working hell. We wear our technology shackles with pride. Managers compete to see whose shackles are the newest and best: tablet, computer, internet service, smart phones and more.

> Management is becoming twenty-first century slavery.

Our ultimate slave drivers are the merciless demands of the market. Our immediate slave drivers are our own bosses. We have a very unequal relationship with them. They matter greatly to us, we are less important to them. If we leave in a huff, complaining about being treated like a slave, we only help make our boss look good: he or she will record that we were not up to the job, did not have the drive and were not a real contributor, so they made the tough decision and let us go. They look like heroes, and we have just become zeroes.

We let ourselves become real slaves to our bosses when we become totally dependent on them. If they are benign slave drivers, they will look after us and make sure we get the good jobs (not cleaning out the lavatories), get well rewarded and, maybe, even get promoted. If they are evil slave drivers, our lives will be a misery.

To buy some freedom, we need to find ways of becoming less than 100 per cent dependent on the whims of our boss. We need some allies and a network of support.

Your career network: checklist

Check your career network against the following:

Sponsors

These will be at least two levels above you in the organisation. They can be critical in nudging your career in the right direction, helping you find the right positions and bosses, and avoiding career traps, providing political air cover when you need to push an agenda item and giving you access to decision makers when you need it. In return, you are their eyes and ears in the organisation, and you may well provide discretionary support and effort on ideas that they are testing and programmes they are starting up. Providing you can continue to add value to them, they will help you. Senior executives often enjoy the energy and alternative perspectives provided by people who do not threaten them. You can make them into your personal coaches with great effect.

Informers

These will let you know what is going on. Particularly valuable are people who know what job opportunities and assignments are emerging.

HR sometimes knows this, but normally there is a grapevine that knows the informal truth long before the official truth comes out. At one bank, staff ran a book on who was going to get promoted or fired next. The odds were very accurate predictors of future events long before HR knew what was happening.

Outsiders

These can help you provide an escape route out of your organisation. Over 70 per cent of executive jobs are both found and filled by word-of-mouth contacts. If you know you can move, you have a much more equal relationship with your boss. If you have nowhere else to go, you are dependent. Professionals in investment banking and in Silicon Valley can command huge salaries, partly because they have great skills, but also because it is very easy in such incestuous industries for them to walk across the road to another organisation: they are not indentured slaves to their current employer.

Ultimately, your security does not come from your employer: it comes from your employability. Make sure that you are building the right skills and right track record for the future. This is your plan B, if things go wrong with your boss. With the right skills and right track record, you will be in demand from people in your network: at minimum they will be ready to recommend you to employers who will want your skills and track record.

Build your skills

At risk of repetition, the skills you need today are not the skills you need tomorrow.

> The skills you need today are not the skills you need tomorrow.

There are two reasons for this.

First, any technical skills you have today are at risk. All skills can become obsolete through changes in technology or in the market. Even if they do not become obsolete, you will find yourself being challenged by younger, hungrier and cheaper talent with the same skill set. Your experience will help for a while, but it becomes ever harder to compete.

Second, the management skills you need to succeed change at each level of the organisation. Look at the table in section 3.10: Learning the right behaviours: what your team really wants in Chapter 3 to see how the demands on a manager change by level.

In the short term, life in the comfort zone is low risk. You stick with the skills you know, you play to your strengths and you do well. In the longer term, life in the comfort zone is fatal. You will find yourself in a skills dead end, being outcompeted by cheaper, younger skills or technology. You have to keep pushing yourself, stretching yourself to learn new skills that will help you build a better future.

Build your claim to fame

We all like to think we are exceptional. There are not many people who would admit to being worse than average at driving, loving, intelligence, achievement or work. At work we are surrounded by people of similar ability to ourselves. They think they are better than us, and we think we are better than them. This logical impossibility is emotionally inevitable.

We need something that easily sets us apart from our colleagues. In a crowded market for promotions, you need to be able to differentiate yourself in some way. Here are three basic ways of achieving differentiation and a claim to fame:

1　**Exceptional achievement.** This has to be demonstrably better than your colleagues. In sales and trading, performance is easy to measure. In many other roles, performance is much more ambiguous.

2　**Starting something**. New initiatives are ever present in most organisations. Not all will succeed, but they offer managers the chance to build a distinctive claim to fame, while learning and growing at the same time.

3 **Changing something**. Managers have to change things and, hopefully, improve them. Failure to change things ranks a manager as an administrator or caretaker. It is not enough simply to do the job: you have to show improvement.

Once you have a claim to fame, you need to stake your claim. If you do not, you will find plenty of people who come out of the woodwork to claim their share of the success you have created. There are simple ways of staking your claim to fame:

- Congratulate and thank people for their contribution. People like public recognition, and you are giving it to them. By congratulating them, you are also showing that you were in the lead role.

- Review and discuss the challenges and lessons learned. This requires a level of knowledge about the initiative, which probably only you have. It demonstrates your mastery of the programme.

- Stay in control and build on success. Take the lead in discussing how to take the initiative to the next stage. This will keep people off your bandwagon because it implies that more work is required (which they do not have time for) and it requires deep knowledge of what is happening, which they lack.

Claims to fame also come whenever you work with top executives. Make a good impression and you have a claim to fame; make a poor impression and you have a claim to infamy. The top executive will judge your track record through the warped lens of their personal experience of you. If you impressed them well, they will interpret your track record favourably. Otherwise, they will regard it suspiciously. This may be unfair, but it is reality. So, you have to make the most of those limited opportunities to meet senior executives. Their limited direct contact with you will influence their thinking more than all the formal HR assessments, which are often exercises in box ticking and propaganda.

Given that moments of truth count, make sure you:

- over-prepare for presentations to top executives. This is your chance to shine, so shine brightly
- act as a role model: positive, professional, proactive
- find opportunities to engage positively with senior executives. These informal opportunities arise all the time: before and after meetings, at conferences, over lunch. Do not hide, shine.

The promotions commission: reality versus reason

We faced a mountain of promotion recommendations. There were over 50 promotion packs of about 40 pages each. We knew that they were as accurate as Pravda in the Soviet era. Each promotion package was a eulogy of unstinting praise. We needed some way of making a decision: 30 promotions were available so there were going to be more than 20 very disappointed people.

We did our best to read the truth behind the propaganda but, inevitably, we always came back to two questions:

1 What has this person really achieved? Every candidate ticked all the boxes in terms of qualifications, teamwork, intellect, leadership and more. But only a few had a real claim to fame that we could recognise. They were easy choices to make.

2 Who knows this person? Often they would be known from a fairly short interaction. Perhaps they had made a presentation or volunteered to do something. If that was a positive event, then the eulogy on paper became more credible. If it was a negative event, we started reading the eulogy much more critically.

In an organisation where everyone appears outstanding, this was the only way we could find of sorting the highest potential from the high potential. We probably got it wrong in some cases, at great human cost. Promotion went to the high PQ managers who had found a claim to fame, staked their claim and taken care to make sure they made a very good impression in even the shortest of contacts with members of the promotions commission.

Act the part

All organisations are tribal: they have their rules and etiquette that all members are expected to follow. These rules vary by level and by function: the culture of sales is usually very different from the culture of accounting. And the culture of new managers is different from the culture of the board room. If you want to join the club, you have to show that you know the club rules and will follow them. We can debate whether such tribalism is good or bad, but we still have to deal with it. That means you have to act the part.

Acting the part is both style and substance. Ultimately, you have to work out the rules for yourself. Some places still believe you have to put your liver on the line to succeed; in others, it seems mandatory to wear ripped jeans and t-shirts. The rules are often bizarre, but you ignore them at your peril.

Below are some common rules that will help you act the part in most places and roles.

Act the part

1 **Set the standard**

   Be a role model to others. Act the way you expect them to act.

2 **Stay positive**

   The harder times are, the more important it is to be positive, confident and supportive. Stand out against others who fall into negativity, blaming, inaction.

3 **Be proactive**

   Find solutions where others find problems; prefer action to analysis; go the extra yard.

4 **Earn respect**

   You do not need to be liked, but you must be respected and trusted. Always deliver, be honest.

▶

5   Maintain guard

Do not play the fool, gossip, bad mouth, betray confidences, get drunk, lose confidential data or indulge in any other career limiting moves (CLMs).

6   Look the part

You should not be judged on how you look, but you will be. Look at how people two levels above you dress and groom: that is the standard to copy.

7   Put etiquette to good use.

Do to others as you would have them do to you; avoid the habits that annoy you in other people.

8   Become a partner, not a servant

If you act like a junior, you will be treated like one. You are not a slave: you are a professional.

9   Follow your role model

If there is someone you admire, do as they do.

10   Follow the rules

This includes knowing when to break the rules.

Control your destiny

The best book you never need to read is called *Control Your Destiny or Someone Else Will* by Noel Tichy and Stratford Sherman. Once you have read the title, you have read the most important message of the book. The rest is detail.

This is the fundamental truth of career management. We have to take control of our destiny, even if that is hard at times. If your career is going wrong, it is easy to rage against the evils of your boss or against the malign forces of fate. These are troubled waters which everyone has to navigate at some point. If you want to find out who is responsible for your fate, look in the mirror.

Career may turn out to be a verb or a noun for you: whichever it is, make the most of it.

4.9 Playing the game: manage the politics

Organisational politics are seen often as a highly dysfunctional game played by dysfunctional managers. This view is often right. But all organisations have politics. Used well, political skills enable managers to make things

> Used well, political skills enable managers to make things happen.

happen through other people and departments. Politics becomes a way of extending the power and capability of each manager. As in *Star Wars*, politics is a force that has a good side and a dark side.

In this section, we will explore the different sorts of games that managers can play, and show how useful each one is. The emphasis of this book is on playing productive political games. The dark side can, indeed, be powerful, but it is very dangerous, and often costly to the organisation as a whole. We will look at three major types of political games:

1 Win/lose games.

2 Appearances games.

3 Performance games.

1 Win/lose games

These are nasty politics played by nasty people. Typically, win/ lose politicians will be found:

● claiming credit for any success with which they can associate themselves

● spreading blame, and finger pointing when anything goes wrong

● gossiping and spreading poison about colleagues.

It can be very tempting to play along with these people. Avoid the temptation. If you do not, you will:

- attract enemies and lose allies fast
- lose credibility and trust when you are found to misrepresent what you have really achieved.

If you encounter nasty politicians, do not play their game to their rules: you are likely to lose. Play to another set of rules – which the politicians cannot win:

- Model professional and positive behaviour: do not get involved in open warfare over who did what when: you will look no better than the politician you are trying to defeat.

- Focus on delivering real performance, not on making big claims: when you achieve something, be generous in your praise of everyone who helped. By giving praise, you stake your claim to being the person at the centre of success, and you gain many allies through your apparent generosity.

- Focus on building your network of trusted allies: people who will help you and whom you will help in return. Do not fight the win/lose politicians directly. They enjoy such fights and, because they have a lot of practice, probably will win.

2 Appearances games

Keeping up appearances is a staple of organisational life. It ranges from the necessary through to the irrelevant or dangerous. In recessions, these games tend to reach fever pitch: everyone wants to look good to avoid the cut when it comes. Here are a few of the games and their value:

- **Facetime game (1).** The first variant of the facetime game is called 'working late, even when there is no work to do'. The idea is to look busy, loyal and committed by staying as late as colleagues and later than the boss. Not good for work–life balance, and a more or less complete waste of time.

In some organisations, however, the facetime game is a necessary evil. At its extreme, it leads to executives stepping off long-haul flights with little sleep and going straight into 12 hours of heavy meetings. Research shows that reaction times of drunks and the sleep deprived are equally bad: yet drunks are fired and the jet-lagged executive is seen to be heroic. Such behaviour is nonsense. Live with it, until the recession blows over, or you can find a better organisation to work for.

- **Facetime game (2).** This variant of the facetime game is about securing invitations to meetings where corporate big shots will be in attendance. This gives the attendee bragging rights with colleagues and may enable him or her to learn more about the big bosses, their agendas and how they work. It does not impress the big bosses to see ranks of mute, wide-eyed junior managers sitting on the fringes of the meeting. If you have something to contribute to the meeting, go. Otherwise find a better use for your time.

- **Facetime game (3).** This is where you descend to leaving jackets on the back of your chair overnight, and similar games, to give the illusion that you are around, even if you are drowning your sorrows in the pub. As soon as your game is rumbled, you lose all credibility: you become a laughing stock for bosses. If you indulge in this sort of behaviour, do not get caught. A safer variant of this game is to check, and reply to, emails last thing at night (preferably not after a long session in the pub): the time stamp on the email will impress your boss with your diligence.

- **Illness game.** This is popular and surprisingly effective. If you have a horrendous bout of flu, turn up at the office and spread your germs to any colleagues or bosses you dislike. You will be sent home in the afternoon to recover. A few months later, when you want to throw a sickie, you can call the office and say you are ill: everyone will believe you because they know from the flu experience that you really do your best to attend work. On the other hand, if you are a committed manager, this is precisely the sort of game you will not play.

● **Dress game**. Books are judged by their covers and managers are judged by their dress. This may be dumb, but it is real: use it to your advantage. If you dress and act like a tramp, you will be treated like one. If you dress and act like people one or two levels above you, you have a chance of being taken seriously, even if your peer group sneers at you. If you want to join the senior management club, observe their rules and rituals and start to apply them to yourself.

3 Performance games

Performance games are a political necessity of organisational life. These are the four essential battles you have to fight, if you are to make progress in the organisation.

1 **Budget battles**. Managers are always encouraged to accept stretching or challenging budgets. In a fit of machismo, some low PQ managers are unwise enough to accept such challenges. That is a recipe for a year of overwork, anxiety and underperformance against expectations that have been set too high. The high PQ manager will fight hard for one or two months of the year to get a sensible budget set in which overperformance, not underperformance, is the likely outcome.

2 **Baseline battles**. These are closely related to budget battles, and they are about setting expectations. When you start in a new position or a new task, set expectations low. Show that the situation you inherited was close to disaster. If your version of events is accepted, anything better than disaster is an improvement. Your predecessor probably will have painted a picture of imminent triumph: living up to those expectations will be nearly impossible. Setting a low baseline and low expectations is standard practice for newly appointed CEOs.

3 **Staff wars**. A-team players make molehills out of mountains.
B-team players are a recipe for overwork, underperformance
and sleepless nights. Play hard to recruit the best members on to
your team and your projects. HR will be keen to give you a toxic
mix of the new and untested, staff who are being given a second
chance and anyone they cannot place elsewhere. By definition,
people you want are probably in great demand and, officially,
will not be available. Invest long hours in wooing them, working
the staffing process and bringing them into your team. It is an
investment of time that will pay you back many times over.

4 **Promotion and bonus battles**. Loyalty is a two-way street.
Managers rightly expect loyalty and commitment from
their teams. In return, team members expect their boss to
deliver at payback time, when it comes to promotions and
bonuses. Inevitably, there will not be enough promotions
or bonuses to satisfy everyone in the organisation. Low PQ
managers understand this and will compromise, much to the
disappointment of their team. High PQ managers will push
their case to the limit on behalf of their team members. Good
teams prefer bosses that look after them, to bosses who put the
organisation before the team.

4.10 Achieving and use influence: become the trusted manager

At the heart of PQ is the idea of influence. Influence allows you
to extend your power beyond your formal limit of authority. This
lets you achieve more by harnessing the power of your colleagues
to make things happen.

Influence is not just about what you do. It is also about how you
are. The way you behave will help you become more or less influential. Your short-hand guide to influence surrounds you at work:
look at who has influence beyond their own area, and see how
they act and behave. They are the role models to follow.

The influential manager is a trusted manager.

Behind the obvious rules of influence lies a deeper rule: the influential manager is a trusted manager. Put it the other way around and it is very hard to become influential if no one trusts you. Without trust, no one will want to work with you, although they may occasionally have to work with you. Trust is the currency of influence: the more trust you acquire, the more influential you can become.

Influence is not about popularity. If you seek popularity, you will find weakness. You make promises, you accept excuses, and you avoid confrontation. In the short term, you may be popular. In the longer term, you become weak and irrelevant. It is better to be trusted and respected than it is to be popular. It is a lesson politicians around the world struggle with.

The best way to destroy trust is to go round saying, 'Trust me...' You cannot claim trust, you have to build trust. Here is a simple way of thinking about how you can build trust, captured in the form of an equation:

$$t = \frac{a \times c}{r}$$

where:

t = trust

a = alignment

c = credibility

r = risk

Here is how you can put these terms to use.

Alignment

We trust people who are like ourselves. This is not good news for diversity, but it is human nature. At work, some people will be like us: they will come from a similar background, share similar tastes, may well be a similar age and same sex and race as ourselves. It is easy to strike up a relationship with such people.

If you find yourself with someone from a completely different background, it is much harder to find any affinity with them. But you can help yourself. Take time to listen to the other person. Let them talk about their favourite subject: themselves. Just the act of listening helps you build a relationship. In a world where everyone is too busy and self-important, it is flattering to have someone listen to what you have to say and to appear interested in your story. Listening also gives you valuable information. It tells you where you may have common interests or experiences. As you discover that you both have more in common than expected, you will start to find some degree of alignment. You have started to build the first building block of trust.

Credibility

Alignment is good, but not enough. When we go out with friends, we will have plenty of alignment in terms of common interests. Whether all your friends would make good colleagues is another matter. We have to know we can rely on them to deliver.

Credibility is about doing as you say. At this point, most people react indignantly and say, 'Well, of course, I always do what I say: you're not implying that I don't keep my word, are you?' Of course, you will be acutely aware of times when peers have failed to deliver to you. And we are all someone else's peer. When we fail to deliver, we sometimes do not even realise it.

There are always reasons why we cannot deliver. Maybe we were let down by someone else: parts were not delivered, analysis we required came too late, and the information was incomplete. In our minds, we have not failed to deliver: someone else has failed to deliver and we are the victims of their incompetence. In the mind of the person to whom we did not deliver, we are the incompetent person who failed to deliver. They do not care about our excuses: all they know is that we did not deliver.

And then there is the question of expectations. Some of the most dangerous words in management are: 'I hope... I will try...

I intend... I may... We could... We might...' In our minds, we have not made any commitment at all, beyond hoping or trying. But, what we say and what is heard are completely different. What is heard is, 'I will...' Later, when we can say we tried, the other person will think, 'You failed.'

This means credibility comes in two parts. The first, obvious part is that we have to deliver. Failure to deliver destroys credibility. Credibility is like a vase: once broken it is hard to put back together again. And excuses are as convincing as repairing a Ming vase with sticky tape.

The less obvious part of credibility is about expectations. We have to be ruthlessly clear about setting expectations. This is difficult. It is human nature to want to please. In the moment, we will use the words 'I hope... I will try...' If you find these words passing your lips, check yourself and ask why you have any doubt about delivering. Then explain your doubts and conditions very clearly. It is better to have a difficult conversation early, that sets expectations clearly, than it is to find excuses later. That is a far harder conversation to have.

Risk

Trust is not an off switch. We have degrees of trust in people. You may trust a stranger in the street to give you directions. You would be unwise to trust a stranger in the street with your life savings. The same applies at work. You have to earn trust step by step. Show that you can deliver on the small things, and slowly you will be trusted to deliver on bigger things.

The alternative way of dealing with risk is to manage it. If you want to take on a risky project, reduce its perceived risk: break it down into small pieces with clear reviews at each step. You may not be trusted with the entire project, but you will be entrusted with each piece of it.

Your network of trust is a vital asset that makes you an effective manager where you work. You discover just how valuable this asset is when you change employer: suddenly you find you have no networks, you do not know who to call on to make things happen, you have no track record and you have to start earning trust and respect all over again. It is seriously hard work.

Influence and trust are invisible advantages, which makes them all the more powerful. Your peers will see you are more effective, but will not quite understand why. They are useful PQ tools: build them, use them.

Chapter 5

Management quotient skills:
managing your journey

Management is an art: it always has been, always will be. There will never be a scientific formula that unlocks the secrets of management in quite the way that $e = mc^2$ unlocked physics. If there was a single formula, we would all have it and we would land up in a competitive stalemate. Everyone would be applying the same formula. Fortunately, people are different, situations are different, actions are different and the world is always changing. There are a million ways to succeed, and as many ways to fail. This makes management the challenge it is. The consequence is that each manager has to learn his or her own rules of survival and success. Any book or course can give a manager only a few more ideas, some different perspectives and a few tools and techniques to try.

> There are a million ways to succeed, and as many ways to fail.

Each person will build his or her own, unique, version of management quotient (MQ). Every manager's success formula will be as unique as their DNA or fingerprints. This means that managers need to acquire three essential MQ skills:

- Acquiring MQ: how to learn success.
- Employing MQ: uses and abuses.
- Decoding the success formula: happy endings.

5.1 Acquiring MQ: how to learn success

Managers are given very little help in becoming managers. Schools teach nothing about political skills and precious little about emotional skills. Arguably, they teach precisely the wrong intellectual skills: they ask students to work alone and produce rational answers to predetermined questions where there is a clear answer. Any manager who expects to work alone, producing rational answers to predetermined questions, is going to have a very short managerial career.

Schools, and business schools, are in the business of teaching explicit knowledge. The problem is that they never teach us how to think. They can teach maths, English, physics and double-entry book-keeping. But thinking simply does not exist as a discipline. It is assumed that if we can do algebra and write a grammatical sentence, then we can think effectively. The evidence of daily life shows that this is a mistake. Alienated youths on the street who resolve disputes by relying on a knife are in the same category as the defensive manager who resolves disputes by relying on authority: neither of them has the mental training to know how to resolve such everyday differences effectively.

The problem continues within organisations. Our research asked managers to pick their two most valuable sources of learning about management from the following list:

● books
● courses
● peers
● bosses
● role models
● experience.

Some 99 per cent of respondents failed to mention books or courses: the only person who really valued books was the only one who had not graduated from high school. This suggests the entire leadership and management development industry is in danger of disappearing in a puff of irrelevance. For an author of a book on management, it is seriously bad news. The challenge is to make any book relevant, readable and practical.

Before discovering how to help people develop their MQ, it is worth looking at how and why current efforts fail. Many organisations offer good professional development in technical skills: helping people learn the trade or craft of their industry, be it law, accounting, bond trading, engineering or accounting. But, when it comes to learning IQ, EQ and PQ, potential participants suddenly discover they are needed elsewhere that day. The Chartered Institute of Personnel and Development (CIPD) found that the most common excuses were:

- they are too busy at work
- family or personal commitments
- they are insufficiently motivated
- resistance from line managers
- insufficient culture of learning at work.

These excuses need a little translation, which is provided below:

- they are too busy at work (= not a priority)
- family or personal commitments (= not a priority)
- they are insufficiently motivated (= not a priority)
- resistance from line managers (= not a priority for the boss)
- insufficient culture of learning at work (= not a priority for anyone).

Lack of time never means lack of time: it means lack of priority. If the same individuals were offered a hot date with their favourite film or sports star and a million pounds, the chances are that they could shuffle their very busy schedules to make the date.

Management training does not quite have the same allure as a hot date and a million pounds for at least two reasons:

1   Most management training is not very good from the participant's perspective.

2   Training assumes that the participant is deficient in whatever they are learning: this is a sign of weakness to which few people care to admit.

Our research shows that most managers learn from peers, bosses, role models and experience. This makes sense to most people. We see someone mess up and quietly make a note not to step on that particular landmine. We see someone else do something really well and, this time, we make a note to try to repeat the trick ourselves. Piece by piece, we beg, borrow and steal little bits of management DNA from the people and events we encounter. The result is that we build up our own unique management DNA, which programmes how we behave under most management situations.

The process of acquiring DNA is highly effective. We do not learn the theory of what should work in general. We learn what works in practice in our particular trade. The investment banker learns to love risk. To civil servants, risk is like kryptonite to Superman: they will do everything to manage it away. The banker and the civil servant are learning opposite lessons and they are both learning the right thing. The practice of what works always trumps the theory of what should work. Practice beats theory every time.

But there is a dark side to this random walk of building your own personalised management DNA. The three major problems are:

● the wrong experiences
● the wrong role models
● the wrong context.

If managers learn from role models and experience, it is essential that they get the right role models and experience.

If they get poor role models and poor experiences, they get poor learning. In every organisation there are a few bosses whose dark reputation precedes them: people *have* to work for them; not many people want to. There are also the nightmare assignments from which few people are expected to escape unscathed.

The random walk of learning from experience can lead to management heaven or management hell, depending on what people and events managers bump into on their journey. There has to be a better way of developing management quotient (MQ).

This book helps the management journey by structuring and accelerating it. Instead of leaving them to learn from random experiences, the book gives managers the frameworks that they need to make sense of what they are seeing, experiencing and learning. For weak managers, frameworks are prisons: they mindlessly apply the same formula, regardless of the circumstances. They are process prisoners and the frameworks are the prison walls. For strong managers, frameworks let them climb the experience curve faster: good frameworks are aids to thinking, not substitutes for thinking.

> Good frameworks are aids to thinking, not substitutes for thinking.

5.2 Employing MQ: uses and abuses

MQ is a simple framework to help you understand the management potential of you and your colleagues. It breaks management down into a set of skills that everyone can learn. These are the skills that managers need to make things happen through other people. By way of summary, here is a simple assessment tool to try on yourself and your colleagues. It tracks the skills outlined in each chapter, so you can refer to the relevant sections, where necessary. How many of the skills can you honestly say you possess at present?

Rational management skills: dealing with problems, tasks and money

1 Start at the end

See the desired outcome for self and for others, simplify issues by focusing on the end and drive towards it.

2 Achieve results

Set clear expectations of what can be achieved by when and deliver them: take responsibility and build a clear claim to fame.

3 Make decisions

Learn what works and what fails in the business (acquire business sense and intuition) and have a bias towards action.

4 Solve problems

Focus on workable solutions, not perfect solutions; solve problems with and through other people, build their buy-in and support in the process.

5 Think strategically

Understand the priorities of senior management and align your personal agenda in support of the broader business agenda.

6 Set budgets

Set realistic expectations upwards, stretching expectations downwards; manage the politics of the budget cycle.

7 Manage budgets

Set expectations early to avoid unpleasant surprises; phase spending to ensure essential investment is made early in the year.

8 Manage costs

Be ready for the year-end squeeze; know where the fat lies; negotiate effectively over any budget revisions.

9 Survive spreadsheets

Understand the key numbers for the business and consistently test and challenge assumptions by using them.

10 Know your numbers

Understand how to use numbers to persuade; use validation process to build buy-in and support for a case.

Emotional management skills: dealing with people

1 Motivate people

Show a real interest in your team and create willing followers.

2 Influence and persuade people

Listen well, understand other people's agendas and build coalitions in support of action by aligning different agendas across the organisation.

3 Coach

Help others discover what works for them; recognise that different people succeed in different ways; do not force your own style on to others.

4 Delegate

Delegate meaningful, stretching tasks as well as routine tasks; set clear and consistent expectations; do not delegate the blame.

5 Handle conflict

Defuse conflict rather than inflame it; recognise which battles are worth fighting and avoid the unnecessary ones.

6 Give informal feedback

Develop team members by giving prompt and positive feedback; move from problems to solutions and action.

7 Use time effectively

Have clear goals and priorities in the short, medium and long term and do not be deflected unnecessarily from them: focus on achievement, not activity.

8 Mind your mind

Be aware of what motivates you; be aware of how you impact others and adjust to different situations and people.

9 Find your performance zone

Retain control of events, even in adversity; rest and relax enough; constantly reflect, learn and grow.

10 Learn the right behaviours

Role model the behaviours most valued in the organisation; be consistently positive, professional and people-focused.

Political management skills: acquiring power to make things happen

1 Find your power sources

Understand how to be of value to the organisation and acquire the relevant capabilities and power to be of value.

2 Acquire power

Build a claim to fame, and stake your claim; actively seek out and ask for or take the appropriate opportunities; do not wait to be asked.

3 Build your power networks

Build alliances with the key power brokers; seek positions that will enhance your long-term career prospects.

4 Use power

Seek power not for status, but for the opportunity to achieve more on a bigger stage; focus on contributions, not rewards.

5 The art of unreasonable management

Know when and how to fight battles and to stretch people beyond their comfort zones.

6 Say no to your boss

Find positive alternatives and use smart questions to get the boss to change direction without having to say no directly.

7 Power and integrity

Build trust based on honesty, even in awkward situations, and on consistent delivery of promises.

8 Take control

Have a clear and compelling vision of what is important, what must change and how it will change.

9 Manage change

Focus on building and maintaining a political coalition in support of change; focus on benefits, business case, actions and outcomes, not on problems; be people-focused more than project-focused.

10 People and change

Manage individuals well through the pain and emotion of change.

Many of these skills will not exist in a formal assessment system, which is why formal assessment systems are so often a source of frustration: they help no one understand what is really important in an effective manager. Although management is everywhere, few people have dared to define it and even fewer teach it: you can learn accounting, finance and marketing and still not know how to manage. This book (and the assessment tool above) helps you cut through the noise and understand the critical skills and interventions every manager needs if they are to succeed in practice.

5.3 Decoding the success formula: happy endings

In 1989 Freddie Mercury and Queen released their album *The Miracle* and sang, 'I want it all and I want it now.' Nowadays, we want more, and we want it faster. This is great news for the modern-day medicine men selling their cure-alls in a bottle. Except that nowadays we are more sophisticated and call the cure things like alternative medicines, holistic treatments or, for businesses, re-engineering, core competences, value innovation and co-creation. We learn the word, take the medicine and... nothing happens.

> Nowadays, we want more, and we want it faster.

People and businesses have been taking quack cures not for decades, but for millennia. We have moved on from sacrificing sheep to the gods, but we still want The Miracle.

The good news for managers is that there is no miracle five-day course that will turn a disillusioned worker into a brilliant manager. You cannot succeed on just five minutes a day, even if there is a promise of your money back. The lack of an instant, universal formula for managerial success is good news for at least three reasons:

1 If there was an instant formula, everyone would have it: you would have no competitive advantage against other managers and you would be left looking for another instant formula to make you stand out.

2 If there was a single formula, management would be a very dull matter of mindlessly applying the same formula day in and day out. There are days when a simple approach would be preferable to the exciting crises of management, but few people would want to do the same thing the same way for 40 or more years.

3   If there was a single formula, we would all have to conform to it like brainwashed zombies. Some managers already behave like brainwashed zombies. The rest of us value being who we are, playing to our strengths and carefully bypassing our (very few and minor) weaknesses.

So, we have to make up our own formula for success. We look, listen and learn from our own experience and from others'. We copy, steal and adapt little bits of management DNA from everyone else. We copy what we like and hope to avoid messing up the way others mess up: we can all find enough creative ways to mess ourselves up without copying other people's faults as well. Eventually, we build up our own unique management DNA, which works in our own unique environment. The perfect manager is as unlikely as the perfect predator: we are as dependent on finding the right context as the polar bear and the lion are.

As we go on our separate management journeys, we need something to help us on our way. This book, any book, cannot pretend to give the universal solution to all management challenges. But, used wisely, it can help you accelerate your learning from experience and, hence, your journey to success.

How to Manage does not give a universal formula for success. It does much better than that. It helps you decode your unique success formula.

Whatever your journey is, enjoy it.

What did you think of this book?

We're really keen to hear from you about this book, so that we can make our publishing even better.

Please log on to the following website and leave us your feedback.

It will only take a few minutes and your thoughts are invaluable to us.

www.pearsoned.co.uk/bookfeedback

Index

Also by Jo Owen

'How to Lead is a tour de force, ambitious and resolutely practical – the very essence of leadership.'
Sharath Jeevan, CEO of STIR Education

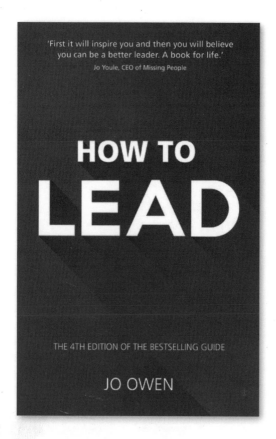

'First it will inspire you and then you will believe you can be a better leader. A book for life.'
Jo Youle, CEO of Missing People

HOW TO
LEAD

THE 4TH EDITION OF THE BESTSELLING GUIDE

JO OWEN

Available at all good bookshops and online at
www.pearson-books.com

 Pearson Business

 @Pearsonbiz